LIKE
A RIVER
TO THE SEA

Heartbreak and Hope in the Wake of United 93

LIKE
A RIVER
TO THE SEA

Heartbreak and Hope in the Wake of United 93

Jack Grandcolas
with Alan Shipnuck

RARE BIRD
LOS ANGELES, CALIF.

RARE BIRD

This is a Genuine Barnacle Book

Rare Bird Books
6044 North Figueroa Street
Los Angeles, CA 90042
rarebirdbooks.com

For more information, address:
Rare Bird Books Subsidiary Rights Department
6044 North Figueroa Street
Los Angeles, CA 90042

Set in Minion
Printed in the United States

10 9 8 7 6 5 4 3 2 1

Library of Congress Cataloging-in-Publication Data

Names: Grandcolas, Jack, author. | Shipnuck, Alan, 1973- author.
Title: Like a river to the sea / by Jack Grandcolas and Alan Shipnuck.
Description: First hardcover edition. | Los Angeles, Calif. : Rare Bird, [2022]
Identifiers: LCCN 2022005720 | ISBN 9781644282229 (hardback)
Subjects: LCSH: Grandcolas, Jack. | Terrorism victims' families—United
States—Biography. | Victims of terrorism—United States. | United
Airlines Flight 93 Hijacking Incident, 2001. | September 11 Terrorist
Attacks, 2001.
Classification: LCC HV6430.G73 A3 2022 | DDC 362.88/9317
[B]—dc23/eng/20220325

LC record available at https://lccn.loc.gov/2022005720

Dear Son…or Daughter,

I am writing this book at the advice of my therapist. She felt it would be helpful to share a little bit about your mom and dad, and why you will always have your place in history. This story may also help others who have suffered a traumatic loss.

Introduction

ON SEPTEMBER 6, 2001, my college sweetheart, Lauren, flew from our home in Northern California to New Jersey. It was a freighted trip. Lauren's dear grandmother, Vivian Catuzzi, had passed away and she was going back east for the funeral. I wanted to go, too, but our old cat, Nicholas, was having health problems. That orange tabby was Lauren's spirit animal. I used to always find them curled up on our bed—Lauren on her tummy, legs in the air like a schoolgirl, reading a book and Nicholas snoozing in a little ball on the small of Lauren's back. Lauren insisted I stay home in San Rafael to take care of the cat. Lauren and I both traveled a fair amount for work, so we were used to saying goodbye, but this parting was one of our most emotional. I was quite fond of Little Grandma, as Vivian was known, and was sorry I couldn't be there to support my wife. But there was also a joyous feeling because Lauren was carrying a secret: she was three months pregnant with our first child, and after Little Grandma's funeral she was planning to share the good news to lift her family's spirits.

We were giddy at the thought of becoming parents, having spent the previous decade trying to get pregnant. There had been plenty of heartbreak along the way, including a miscarriage in 1999, when Lauren was thirty-six. Two years later, we had pretty much resigned ourselves to raising only cats…and then a miracle happened.

On her last night in New Jersey, Lauren called and gave me an enthusiastic recounting of the big reveal of her pregnancy. I always loved talking to her on the phone—she had the cutest little voice, so full of life, and especially so on this night. She and her sisters were about to watch a movie, with Lauren having prepared her favorite snack: a bowl of popcorn mixed with steamed vegetables. I promised I would be there to pick her up at the airport the next day—September 11.

Our house had two stories and we slept upstairs. (The nursery was to be just down the hall.) Those were the days of intrusive calls from telemarketers, so I turned off the ringer on the phone in our bedroom and fell asleep with a smile on my face.

I was awakened early the next morning by the distant sound of the answering machine in the kitchen downstairs. I rolled over and snoozed a little more. When I opened my eyes again, they went right to the clock: 7:03. And then the damnedest thing happened. I looked out of the bay window facing the bed and saw a spirit. Even now it seems unbelievable, but I know what I saw: the shape of an angel, opaque around the edges as if glimpsed through a drop of water, rising toward the heavens and out of view. I laid in the bed for a few moments, overwhelmed. All I could think of in that moment was, *Whom do I know that recently died?* Then it occurred to me that perhaps it was Little Grandma. Back then, I was not a spiritual person, but I felt humbled and grateful to have been visited by this otherworldly being.

I floated out of bed, checked on the cat, and then turned on the television news, my usual morning routine. I began shaving but was distracted by the confounding sight on the TV of smoke pouring out of both Twin Towers. The awful images kept coming: suddenly the Pentagon was on fire, and then reports that a plane was down in the Pennsylvania countryside. Like every American, I was sickened by what I was watching. But I wasn't worried about my wife. The TV commentators said that planes had been grounded nationwide and my first instinct was that Lauren was stuck at Newark. My initial concern was for my older brother, Jim, a pilot for American Airlines who often flew out of New York and Boston. The phone rang and I expected it to be Lauren with an update. It was her sister, Vaughn, with whom she had been staying.

"Is Lauren with you?" I asked.

"No, she left early," Vaughn said, and a little current of panic ran through me. "I haven't heard from her. I thought she might've contacted you."

I answered, "No! I thought she would return to your house since her flight was grounded?"

That's when Vaughn said something that made my hair stand on the back of my neck, "Lauren called and told me she was able to get on an earlier flight."

At that moment, another call came in. I was praying it was Lauren, but instead I heard the voice of my friend Bob Schultz. "I was worried about you, Rackster," he said, invoking an old nickname. "I know you travel to New York a lot." I told him about Lauren flying home from Newark and that I was becoming concerned since I had not yet heard from her. That was when I remembered the answering machine. I bolted downstairs and saw the flashing red light indicating a new message.

Lauren was one of those people who always cut it close getting to the airport but was so charming in her apologies you could never be mad at her. That morning she had been booked on a 9:20 a.m. flight from Newark to San Francisco but somehow arrived at the airport early enough to be asked if she'd like a seat on a flight that was scheduled to depart an hour and twenty minutes earlier: United 93. The first message was Lauren calling me from Newark to inform me of the change to her itinerary, though she didn't mention the flight number. Listening to her sweet voice, I could feel my heart pounding. I shouted out, "Please be okay. Please be okay!" On the TV were images of a smoldering hole in the ground in the Pennsylvania countryside. At that moment the commentators were saying they believed that plane had originated in Chicago, and I breathed a huge sigh of relief…but where was Lauren? The next message played. It was her calling from the plane; in those days there were credit card–activated phones hardwired to the seat backs.

Lauren had worked as a marketing manager at PricewaterhouseCoopers. It was a high-pressure job, and she was often surrounded in the boardroom by alpha males in Brooks Brothers suits. But she was utterly unfazed because her father, Larry, had been a football coach and she grew up on the sidelines among all that testosterone. Lauren was a standout tennis player in high school and ever after embraced pressure moments; for a big meeting with Nick Graham, the founder of Joe Boxer, Lauren convinced all her dubious male colleagues to don colorful Joe Boxer underwear over their gray flannel suit pants, and Graham was so tickled by the stunt he hired PwC on the spot. So, it was no surprise that on the answering machine Lauren's voice was clear and strong, almost businesslike. "*Honey, are you there? Jack? Pick up, sweetie. Okay, well, I just want to tell you I love you. We're having a little problem on the plane. I'm fine and comfortable and I'm okay for now. I just love you more than*

10

anything, just know that. It's just a little problem, so I, I'll…Honey, I just love you. Please tell my family I love them, too. Bye, honey."

I fell to the ground and began sobbing. In that moment I knew Lauren and our baby were gone. The next time I looked at the TV, the crash site in Shanksville, Pennsylvania, was being shown and the announcers were saying that early reports indicated the downed plane was United 93 out of Newark. There didn't appear to be any survivors.

Later, I would find out that Lauren's plane fell to the earth at 10:03 a.m. That's 7:03 in California. The angel that visited me in the sky through the bedroom window wasn't Little Grandma. It was Lauren.

1

I WAS BORN IN Belleville, Illinois, in 1962. It's a quiet little town but I created some excitement at age four: I found fifty cents in the couch cushions, snuck out the back door, and walked a couple of miles to the only McDonald's in town. I can still remember looking up at the befuddled cashier while ordering my cheeseburger and chocolate shake. Then I walked all the way home, carrying my little bag with the cheeseburger inside. When I came home, my brother Jim—who was supposed to have been watching me—didn't ask where I'd been, merely how I had scrounged up the money for McDonald's. When I told him, he claimed the wayward fifty cents had been his. As payback, Jim snatched away the cheeseburger and scarfed it down, leaving me in tears. When you're the youngest of six, you learn to be independent and to take your lumps.

A year later we moved to Muncie, Indiana, the so-called Middletown, USA, where my father, Leon, took a job as controller at the Ball Corporation. As a young man he was a marine who fought in the South Pacific during World War II. I think he always carried those scars. He was certainly not the type of father who ever said "I love you," but he was there whenever I needed him. I would seek him out in his La-Z-Boy in the bedroom and he would put down the paper and listen intently to whatever was on my mind. Dad's advice was always simple and profound, and to this day I still repeat one of this old accountant's favorite sayings: "Worrying is like paying interest on a debt you don't owe." Mom was active and spirited and ever the prankster. She taught me that all people have value, regardless of their background.

When my friends and I weren't jumping off one-hundred-foot cliffs into the rock quarries or "bumper-hopping" on icy roads while clinging to the back of speeding cars, organized sports was a big part of my youth. I played basketball and football, but golf was where I really excelled; I won my first junior club championship when I was nine, beating kids who were two and three years older. My dad shared a love for the game and we played many rounds together. When I was twelve, we were watching the Crosby Clambake on TV. It was snowy and miserable in Muncie, and I was mesmerized by the images of Pebble Beach on the screen, with the green grass and blue ocean glittering in the sunshine. All the pros and their amateur partners were wearing stylish clothes and having a great time and I said to Dad, "I want to be one of those guys someday. How do I get there?"

"Work hard, save, and invest your money," he said. Those words were burned into my memory.

I continued to excel at golf as I reached my teenage years. Three times I was chosen to play in the Tri-State Invitational, which brings together top players from Ohio, Indiana, and Kentucky. In 1979, I qualified for the US Junior Amateur Championship in Hilton Head, South Carolina. A local family was gracious enough to let me stay in their home and their ten-year-old son turned into my shadow. He was such a sweet kid

I let him caddie for me in the tournament and his enthusiasm for my game gave me a shot of confidence. I played well against a field of the best junior amateurs in the country and that helped me realize that golf could be my ticket out of Indiana. When it was time to go away to college, I chose the University of Texas. My brother Mark was an alumnus and had told me plenty of stories about a great school in a fun town teeming with beautiful coeds. The warm weather in Austin was appealing, too, as it would allow me to work on my game year-round. I earned a spot on the freshman golf team. Only the five best players on the squad secured a place in the tournament lineup and I was always on the fringe, which made every round stressful. I thought my dream was to join the likes of upperclassmen Mark Brooks, Brandel Chamblee, and Lance Ten Broeck on the varsity squad, but after one season I realized they were at a different level, skill-wise, and that I was burnt-out from all those years of junior golf. I left the team and embarked on a double major of communications and partying.

During my sophomore year, in 1983, I took a course in government studies with a friend of mine from Sigma Phi Epsilon. Walking into the classroom on the first day we bumped into a high school friend of his from Houston: Lauren Catuzzi. He introduced us and I vividly remember thinking, *Oh, my god, these are the most beautiful blue eyes I've ever seen.* She had a cute smile, too, and such a spirit about her. I was immediately smitten but had a girlfriend at the time. Still, whenever I would run into Lauren around campus, we had an undeniable spark. One of her friends even told me she thought we would be perfect together.

After I broke up with my girlfriend, I called Lauren one night under the guise of looking for my friend who was dating her roommate. I knew full well he wasn't there, but I wanted to chat with Lauren. I was too nervous to actually ask her out, but we had a nice conversation and I felt a rare ease with her. She mentioned that she was interested in a band I'd never heard of called U2. They were coming to town soon, so I bluffed that I had access to tickets and then worked feverishly to actually get them in hand. Lauren was euphoric when I told her. On the night of the concert, I showed up at her place with a bottle of wine and a bouquet of flowers. She had left the apartment door open for me. When I tapped on the doorframe, she was brushing her teeth so she called out, "The money's on the counter, just leave the ticket." I was still standing there, dumbfounded, when Lauren came out of the bathroom. Seeing me with the flowers and the wine was her first inkling that I wanted to take her on a date, not just serve as a ticket broker. She paused and then said, "Oh, it's a date. That's great!" After that awkward start, we had a blast at the concert. She adored Bono and I loved listening to Lauren belt out the words to every song. We quickly fell hard for each other.

It turns out that Lauren also had Hoosier roots but spent most of her childhood in New Jersey before going to high school in Houston, Texas. This tracked with the career arc of her father, who was an assistant football coach at Indiana, then at Ohio State under Woody Hayes, and finally with the Houston Gamblers of the ill-fated USFL. Along the way, Coach (as everyone who knew Larry referred to him) helped popularize the lonesome polecat formation, in which the quarterback was alone in the backfield, allowing for more wide receivers and sophisticated offensive sets. Lauren had great stories about growing up in football, including the time she played a game of catch with Terry Bradshaw and Lynn Swann before an exhibition game when her dad was an assistant coach for the Baltimore Colts.

I heard all the tales about Lauren's childhood. She was a fun, quirky kid, who at age four asked Santa Claus for only one thing: her very own bottle of ketchup. As the middle of three sisters, she had to fight for attention; she once decided to run away from home but only made it as far as the neighbor's house, where she knocked on the door and asked for milk and cookies. When she got a little older, Lauren delighted in the awkwardness of elevator rides. Her younger sister Vaughn recalls, "She would speak into the silence something bizarre like, 'Hey, did that blister ever heal up?'" Lauren was a chameleon who moved effortlessly through the different cliques of her schools. "From the jocks to the 'brains' to the popular girls— of which she was one—to the nerds and especially to the quiet souls," says Vaughn. "She had a gift that allowed her to truly get to know people and become part of their lives. Starting with her beautiful smile, people just gravitated toward her radiant personality and genuine thoughtfulness." She could also disarm you with her sense of humility.

Lauren had a mischievous streak. Since Coach was an old-school tough guy, she decided to play a prank on him the first time him and I were to meet. I reluctantly went along with it. Lauren had me wear a dangly earring and eyeliner, and found a red shirt that looked like it had been stolen from Michael Jackson's closet. When we finally met up for cocktails at the bar of Coach's hotel, he couldn't disguise his horror. I've never felt more ridiculous, but the woman we both loved laughed about it for years afterward, which made it well worth it. Coach and I would play many rounds of golf together and came to be quite close. I admired him for the way he navigated the waters of a very female household. Later, Lauren and I would travel with her parents. Her mom, Barbara, had a wicked sense of humor.

I loved both of them and being a part of the Catuzzi family. There were always lots of laughs and Lauren was usually at the center of it all.

But there was also a serious side to her. Lauren was passionate about women's rights and interned for Governor Ann Richards as an undergrad. Back then I was a conservative Republican and she was a very liberal Democrat, but it worked because she had so much conviction I enjoyed hearing her side of every issue, even when I didn't agree.

I was a year ahead of Lauren in school. After earning my degree in 1985, I took a job in Northern California doing marketing for a semiconductor company. With her still in Austin, we made the hard decision to take some time apart. But dating other people only made us miss each other more. When Lauren graduated, she moved to San Francisco so we could be together again. We picked up right where we had left off.

I didn't love my job so, on my dad's advice, I started networking. I was interested in the media business so I wrote letters to top sales executives at places like *Sports Illustrated*, *Time, Forbes, Fortune, Business Week*, and *USA Today*. I said I was not looking for a job, just requesting fifteen minutes to ask about their career and how they had prospered. It turns out that everyone likes talking about themselves, so a surprising number of these busy people agreed to meet. Dad offered very specific instructions: "Buy some nice Allen Edmonds patent leather shoes, a Halston suit, a white shirt, and a set of ties and go out there and show them that you want to be professional." I did as instructed. After each meeting, I would follow up with a hand-written thank you note. This made enough of an impression on some folks at *USA Today* that I was granted a second meeting and then a chance to pitch them on a project a couple of weeks later as an audition for a sales manager job in San Francisco. As I was preparing for that big break, I blew out my ankle playing basketball. At my apartment I hobbled around on crutches, practicing my presentation. These were the days of flip charts, and it was a struggle to manage that on crutches while still trying to offer a dynamic presentation. At one point I vented to Lauren that I didn't think I could do it. I wanted to cancel the presentation, citing my injury. With some steel in her voice she said, "You can do it and I'm going help you." That was so Lauren. She was always extremely positive, and her attitude uplifted everyone around her. She pushed me hard to perfect the presentation, and when the time came, I nailed it, despite the crutches. I got hired as an ad sales executive at *USA Weekend,* the Sunday supplement carried by newspapers all over the country. I busted my butt and a year later was promoted to a sales manager position at *USA Today*. None of that would have happened without Lauren's tireless support.

She was also making her way in the business world. Lauren had started working for a law firm right out of college but then took a job at PricewaterhouseCoopers, which tickled my family because that's where my dad began his career. Lauren may have been a petite little thing with a soft voice, but she more than held her own in the boardroom. "She had a presence," says Nick Graham. "We were looking for a CPA for Joe Boxer and interviewed a lot of different firms. As you can imagine, these guys were all very serious. Lauren was a sparkle in a gray flannel world. She was engaging, she was happy, she was keenly interested in what we wanted and what we needed. She got our vibe, that we wanted to do things a little differently. She is the reason I hired PwC."

Lauren was always trying to better herself, so she went through the training to become a certified emergency medical technician. She didn't aspire to work in that field, she just wanted to be able to help people in distress should she ever be needed. Sure enough, she saved a man's life at a Dallas health club by performing the Heimlich maneuver as he choked on a piece of gum. She rescued a woman whose foot got trapped in an escalator at a department store and tended to an injured motorist who drove into a ditch near our home. In all of these moments what struck onlookers about Lauren was her coolness under fire and a willingness to jump into the fray wielding instructions and care.

I had my own experiences that showed me how fragile life can be. My lifelong best friend, John Barnes, died at age thirty-two of a rare stomach cancer. He was such a sweet, caring soul and the passion with which John lived inspired me to try to do the same. One weekend in 1989, my brothers, some friends, and I decided to sail to the Channel Islands, off the coast of Santa Barbara. We were going to spearfish and just relax in the sun. As we were preparing to set sail, under a bright morning sun, we heard a report on the radio that a search-and-rescue mission had just been called off for a pair of sea urchin fishermen who had disappeared near the islands days before. A little chill went down my spine, but the weather was perfect and we merrily set sail. On our first evening, we scrambled up the cliffs to watch the sunset. There were no other boats in view but across the bluffs we spotted a lone figure, walking unsteadily toward us. As he got closer, we could see it was a disheveled young man. He was one of the missing fishermen. He told us his name was Mark and we took him back to our boat, fed and clothed him, and he haltingly told us his story. Two nights earlier, Mark's boat had been swamped by twelve-foot swells. His fishing buddy was washed overboard. Mark was able to put on his dry suit before the boat sank, and he floated for many hours atop a surfboard, going in and out of consciousness. He was at the mercy of the tides but eventually washed ashore on the Channel Islands. A day later, he saw our boat arrive and he scrambled across the island to intercept us. After hearing his story, we radioed the Coast Guard for help and they sent a helicopter to whisk Mark back to shore, leaving us in a haze of elation and disbelief. Two days later, we pulled back into the marina in Santa Barbara and Mark was waiting for us, along with his wife, baby, and four-year-old son. His wife hugged me, then looked into my eyes and said, "You were an angel sent from God." I don't know about all that, but her words always stayed with me as a reminder that every day people can find themselves in the most extraordinary circumstances.

LAUREN AND I WERE having a blast living together in San Francisco and got engaged in June 1990, at our favorite restaurant on Union Street. A year later we were married at the Hamlin Mansion, a grand old estate with sweeping views from atop Pacific Heights. Unfortunately, the gal who normally did Lauren's hair fell ill and had to cancel at the last minute. When I laid eyes on my bride-to-be for the first time on our wedding day, I had to hide my shock—her fill-in hairdresser had given her a towering bouffant that was unlike any hairstyle I'd even seen on Lauren. "Don't say anything about my hair," she whispered to me. "I spent the last hour crying." Still, it was a lovely wedding and I felt like the luckiest guy in the world. We took a honeymoon to St. Barts in the Caribbean.

Upon our return, there was a corporate restructuring and I parted ways with *USA Today*, so we lit out for Europe for three months for a *second* honeymoon. We loved exploring other cultures and tried to help correct the impressions that many folks over there had about Americans. We made many friends along the way and came to realize that, despite the cultural differences, we shared a common humanity.

Once home, Lauren challenged herself to continue learning new things and deepen her understanding of the world. She recalled the merit badges she earned as a young Girl Scout and wanted to continue that striving into adulthood. "Why would someone ever want to stop growing?" she would ask me. Lauren became involved in charitable fundraisers for everything from AIDS and cancer research to animal welfare. She took scuba lessons, knowing it was a passion of mine, and we had some unforgettable undersea adventures. As her thirtieth birthday approached, Lauren said she wanted to do something big but she wouldn't tell me what. Lauren was fiercely protective of loved ones and never wanted anyone to worry about her. So, it wasn't until the morning of her birthday, in 1993, that she announced we were going skydiving. I think from the look on my face she could tell I was a little apprehensive, so she added, "Well, I'm going skydiving—you don't have try it." Our friend Glenn Anderson was flying in that day from Alaska. We picked him up at the airport and with a twinkle Lauren told him our next stop was the skydiving airfield. Glenn is a big, gregarious outdoorsman who works in radio. He's never short on words but now he got a little wide-eyed. After a long pause, Glenn said, "I just got off a perfectly good airplane, why would I wanna go up in another smaller one and jump out of it?!" Those were my feelings exactly. When we arrived at the skydiving place, Lauren couldn't contain her excitement. Glenn and I weren't planning to jump but, seeing the fearlessness of this little cutie pie, I finally said to him, "What kind of wimps are we?" So, thanks to Lauren's example, we also took the plunge. For the video of the jumps, Lauren chose her favorite U2 song, "One Tree Hill," to serve as the soundtrack. She always gave it a little extra when singing the chorus, *we run like a river to the sea.* I've watched that video many times and it's always striking to hear those words as Lauren's chute opens and she ascends into the shining sunlight.

∾

AFTER LEAVING *USA TODAY*, I took a job with Prodigy, one of the first online services. The internet was in its infancy, but it was already becoming clear the business world would be profoundly affected. In 1995, I was offered the job of national director of high-tech sales for the Newspaper National Network, which centralized advertising for big corporations across dozens of the country's biggest papers, allowing me to work with friends and contacts at some of the largest Fortune 500 companies. Business was booming and we wound up buying a house north of San Francisco in the town of San Rafael. (I had never forgotten Dad's mantra: *Work hard, save, and invest your money.*) We wanted the extra space because we were ready to have a family.

When you tell your buddies that you're trying to get pregnant, there are always lots of jokes about that being good work if you can get it, but in fact it's nerve-wracking. I think the stress has a negative effect on the body, which makes it that much harder for nature to take its course. Eventually we discovered Lauren had a blocked fallopian tube and she had surgery to correct that. But her other tube had some damage that couldn't be fixed, and we were told that put Lauren at risk of an ectopic pregnancy, which made us even more unnerved. She finally got pregnant in 1999, at age thirty-six. We were over the moon, but within a few weeks she miscarried. That was a heavy time. We had some tough conversations, really questioning if we would be happy together with just cats, or if we wanted to begin the complicated process of trying to adopt.

All of that reflecting helped push Lauren to pursue her longtime ambition of writing a book. She continued her job on the marketing side at *Good Housekeeping* but devoted more and more of her time to the book. It was focused on encouraging women to achieve their dreams at work and in their personal lives. She had the clever idea of using the Girl Scouts' merit badge system as a way to track these achievements. I loved watching her make list after list of ideas for the book. It was truly a labor of love.

Of course, as we became more peaceful with the idea of not being parents, that was when Lauren got pregnant again. We didn't tell a soul, knowing full well the delicateness of her condition. Keeping that secret made us feel closer than ever. But then Little Grandma died.

Lauren's flight to New Jersey on September 6, 2001, was quite early and she sneaked away without disturbing me. When I woke up, I was a little upset that I didn't get to give her a goodbye kiss. I'm not sure why, but the more I thought about it the more bothered I became. It was a tension and anxiety I had never felt before. Eventually I calmed myself with the simple thought that I would be kissing her again in only a few days.

2

AFTER LISTENING TO LAUREN'S message on the answering machine, I was still on the floor bawling when the phone rang. I lunged for it, hoping against hope she was calling. But it was my friend Mike Collins, who had been over for dinner the night before. We watched *Monday Night Football* and played cards deep into the night. Maybe it was the wine talking, but we'd had a heartfelt discussion about being grateful for our charmed lives. Now Mike was calling to share his disbelief at the unfolding horrors. "Are you watching this?" he said. "I was supposed to be on a flight to New York today, but they turned me around at the gate and…"

I stopped him and said, "Lauren was on one of the planes that crashed. She's gone."

There was a long pause, and then Mike said, "We'll be right over."

Within minutes, he and his wife, Kathy, arrived and enveloped me in a hug. We stood there crying and embracing for a very long time.

I paced back and forth in the living room, unable to stop, unable to think clearly. I know now that I was in clinical shock—my breathing was weak and shallow, I had a cold, clammy sweat going, and I felt faint to the point of dizziness.

It was overwhelming trying to process my private heartbreak along with our national tragedy. We were clearly at war but only one side knew why. There were so many unanswered questions, but all I cared about in that moment was, *Why had they taken my sweet Lauren? And our baby?* I tried not to picture her final moments, but it was impossible to keep those terrifying thoughts at bay. Waves of nausea overcame me. There were times when I felt like I was suffocating. Periodically I bent over at the waist, with Mike and Kathy rubbing my back, trying to get me to breathe. Lauren was my whole world. We had been through so much together. How could she be gone, just like that? Our future with the baby had been laid out so clearly in my mind. Before Lauren left for New Jersey, we had even settled on names: Grace if it was a girl, Gavin if it was a boy. We were picking paint colors for the nursery. Now I would never get to hold this child, to love and protect it. The survivor's guilt hit me right away. I had dedicated my life to taking care of Lauren, but at the moment she needed me the most, I wasn't there for her. Other emotions came on unexpectedly; at one point I said to Mike, "I can't believe I'm a widower." It's such a strange, old-fashioned word. That was me now, at the age of thirty-eight. Everything I knew and loved had been taken while I slept.

I'm not sure how word spread so quickly, but within an hour my house was full of two dozen friends. No one knew what to say, but there was comfort in the solidarity. There was a knock at the door and suddenly two FBI agents were in my living room. They asked to speak privately and, for the first time, I had confirmation of what I already knew in my heart: according to the passenger manifest, Lauren was aboard United 93, the plane that had crashed in the Pennsylvania countryside. There were no survivors. The agents explained that the plane's takeoff had been delayed at Newark by about forty-five minutes, which is how those on board knew that the other planes had crashed into the Twin Towers and Pentagon. Information was still sketchy, but there was some indication that there had been an uprising among the passengers and crew in an attempt to retake control of the plane from the hijackers. The agents asked if Lauren had contacted me, so I played for them her voice message. We listened to it a few times. These agents were big, serious, tough-looking guys, but both had tears in their eyes. They remarked how calm and brave she sounded. That was when I first felt the power of Lauren's words. During the scariest moment of her life, she sent a message of love and comfort. Her plane had been hijacked but she didn't want *me* to be worried. It was the last selfless act of a deeply compassionate woman.

My old-fashioned answering machine recorded the messages on a mini-cassette tape. The agents asked to take the tape with them, saying that with the equipment at their field office they could amplify the background noises and conversations and perhaps glean information about what had transpired aboard the airplane. Already I was feeling protective of Lauren and her memory so I told them I wouldn't surrender the tape unless they promised in writing that the message would not be released publicly. They couldn't do that, so I said no. The agents were very professional and courteous, and they accepted my wishes. They left a short while later. I hadn't realized that a couple of my friends were lingering in the doorway and heard the exchange. With wide eyes, one of them said, "Dude, I can't believe you just stared down the FBI." I was so numb it hadn't even registered.

Things were happening fast now. A couple of TV trucks began setting up in front of the house, so I sent out a friend with a message requesting privacy. My phone wouldn't stop ringing, so I deputized another person to take messages. Feeling overwhelmed, I lay down on the couch and asked not to be disturbed. But a short while later, I got word that Lauren's father was on the phone, hoping to speak to me.

Coach greeted me as always, saying, "Hey, Jack, how are ya?" As soon as I heard his chipper voice, I was flooded with an awful realization: *He doesn't know*. It turned out that Lauren's parents had left early that morning to drive from New Jersey to their second home in Asheville, North Carolina. With the radio off and minimal cell reception, they were shielded from all that had happened. There is no way to prepare for having to tell two loving parents that their little girl is gone forever. In that moment I could feel all the acid from my stomach travel to my throat. "I'm not good, Coach," I said.

"What's wrong?"

"Lauren's plane went down. There were no survivors."

All these years later, the sounds that followed are burned into my memory. Coach shouting, "No, no, no!" and then, after he said something to Barbara, her anguished wailing. "We're going to pull over and I'll call you back," he said. I dropped the phone and my tears came yet again.

The rest of that day is a blur. I spoke to Lauren's sisters and to my family, with my mom promising to drive up the next day to come stay with me. I couldn't handle seeing the horrific images on the television, but friends periodically informed me of what was being learned about the attacks. Someone organized dinner and it was my first food of the day; it hadn't occurred to me to have a bite to eat. How was I supposed to focus on such things? It's like somebody rips open your chest, grabs your heart, tears it in half, shoves it back in, stitches you up, and says, "Okay, carry on." I didn't know how to do that. Not yet.

Still, a couple of days later I stepped in front of the cameras on my front porch and, with my family by my side, read a prepared statement. I really just wanted to crawl into a hole and hide but having worked in the newspaper industry for so long I have a lot of respect for reporters, and I knew they were just doing their job. Complicating my grieving process was that all of America was in mourning, too. Lauren was now much more than my lost sweetheart—she was part of a story of historical importance, the magnitude of which was still being revealed. She had become part of the public domain. And yet in the quiet moments when the house was empty, I had her memory all to myself. I would bury my face in the pillows of our bed so I could still smell Lauren. The hairs in her brush made me smile because it was a tangible part of her that remained. I would look at the photos and speak out loud to her. I even found myself in the closet hugging her clothes, breathing her in. I was desperate to feel close to Lauren because I knew someday her scent would fade away forever.

$\sim$

LAUREN'S FUNERAL WAS HELD at a Catholic church in Houston. It was standing room only, with easily 600-plus people on hand to pay their respects. I had told her family ahead of time that I didn't think I could speak. It was still too raw. But as we gathered at the church, Coach approached me and said I'd have to get up and say a few words because he no longer felt capable of doing so. That was a gut punch, but what choice did I have? I loved Coach and Lauren and their family, and now I had to come through for all of them. I barely heard the priest's sermon because I was in my own head, trying to collect my thoughts.

The skies were dark and gloomy, matching all of our moods. Thunder boomed in the distance. Waiting to be called up to speak, I felt frozen in the pew. In desperation I started praying to Lauren, saying the words quietly so no one could hear: "Darling, I don't know if I can do this. I don't know how I'm gonna do this. Give me some strength. Please!" And just then a small beam of green light came through the stained glass, fixing its glow upon me. I looked around to see if anyone else was receiving this light, but it was just me. And then I felt Lauren speaking to me: *You can do this. I want you to get up there and show them what a great guy I chose to marry. Do it for me and all the hometown folks. I'm here to help you.* When I stood up to speak, my legs buckled and I wasn't sure I'd make it to the podium. But I got up there and poured my heart out as to who Lauren was and how dearly she would be missed. When I looked out at all those faces, it seemed like tears streaked every cheek. Afterward a few people told me they were inspired by my strength. But it wasn't mine—whatever courage I had was borrowed from Lauren.

3

ABOARD UNITED 93 THERE were thirty-three passengers, five flight attendants, and the captain and copilot. (I choose not to include the hijackers in my count.) They were brought together by fate. Like Lauren, Tom Burnett was originally booked on United 91, which was scheduled to leave at 9:20 a.m., but he arrived early enough at Newark to get a seat on United 93, which was to depart at 8:00 a.m. Tom was the CEO of a medical device company, with a wife and three young daughters at home in San Ramon, California. Donald and Jean Peterson—the only married couple on the flight—also switched to United 93 from 91. Others booked it at the last minute, made possible because there were so many empty seats on the Boeing 757-222, which could accommodate 182 passengers. Nicole Miller had tried to fly out the day before on US Airways, but her plane was grounded for hours by thunderstorms. She decided to try again the next morning. When she couldn't get a seat on her boyfriend, Ryan Brown's, Northwest Airlines flight to San Jose, Nicole booked a spot on United 93. Mark Bingham was supposed to return home to San Francisco on September 10, but after a big night out celebrating a friend's birthday, he pushed back his flight by twenty-four hours. Wanda Green was a United flight attendant who wasn't due to work again until September 13, but this single mother of two switched her shift to United 93 so she could get to San Francisco earlier in order to close a deal in her other job as a realtor.

Every passenger had a unique reason for being on the plane—some tragic, some uplifting, some mundane. John Talignani, a retired bartender, was traveling to California to collect the remains of his stepson, who had died in a car accident on his honeymoon. Deora Bodley was heading back to Santa Clara University for her junior year after having spent the summer as an aide in a second-grade classroom. Alan Beaven had been living in an ashram in upstate New York with his wife, Kimi, and five-year-old daughter, Sonali; an environmental lawyer, he was headed to San Francisco to dispose of one final Clean Water Act case before beginning a yearlong sabbatical that was to include conservation work outside of Mumbai.

All of these strangers sat together on the runway at Newark. Because of congestion at the airport, United 93 didn't take off until 8:42 a.m. Five minutes later, American Airlines flight 11 crashed into the North Tower of the World Trade Center. Early reports were that a small private aircraft had struck the skyscraper; a tragic accident, to be sure, but not cause for widespread concern. Camera crews rushed to the southern tip of Manhattan to film smoke pouring out of the tower, and numerous commuters and tourists captured the scene on their phones or cameras. At 9:02 a.m., United 93 reached its cruising altitude of 35,000 feet. One minute later, United Airlines 175 slammed into the South Tower traveling at nearly 600 miles per hour. The images were beamed around the world in real-time. In the shock and confusion only one thing was clear: we were under attack.

The men flying United 93—Captain Jason Dahl and First Officer LeRoy Homer, Jr.—were not immediately aware of the unfolding events. It wasn't until 9:23 a.m. that a warning was sent to the plane informing the pilots that two planes had struck the Twin Towers and to be aware of a possible cockpit intrusion. At 9:26 a.m., Dahl confirmed receipt of the message. Two minutes later the hijackers stormed the cockpit, wielding razor-sharp box cutters that were allowed as carry-ons under the lax security regulations of that era. The terrorists had received extensive training from Al-Qaeda operatives in Afghanistan in early 2001; they were made to butcher a sheep and a camel to learn how to wield a knife. The FAA air traffic control center in Cleveland received transmissions from the cockpit, capturing the sounds of an intense physical struggle and the following dialogue: "Hey, get out of here. Get out of here! Get out of here! Mayday!" Both Dahl and Homer were stabbed, sustaining grave injuries. The plane dropped 700 feet before being stabilized. By 9:32 a.m., the terrorists had taken control of United 93. One of them, believed to be Ziad Jarrah, made an announcement on the intercom in imperfect English: "Ladies and gentlemen, here the captain. Please sit down, keep remaining seating. We have a bomb on board. So sit." It was not immediately clear to those on board if the captain and copilot had been killed, injured, or otherwise subdued, but passenger Todd Beamer told a GTE-Verizon operator that two men were lying on the floor of the first-class cabin, and they were believed to be Dahl and Homer.

Within minutes, the 757 banked hard to the left and began traveling southeast, on a collision course with Washington, DC, though the passengers didn't yet know that was the destination. They had been herded to the back of the airplane where many immediately began making calls on the GTE-Verizon phones that were hardwired to the seat backs. (Later, the plane would fly so low that passengers picked up reception on their cell phones.) Tom Burnett reached his wife, Deena, saying the hijackers had stabbed a man who had been seated in first class. He told her that one of the terrorists was wielding a bomb. Deena informed her husband of the attacks on the World Trade Center.

"Oh, my God," Tom said. "It's a suicide mission."

He shared the news with passengers seated nearby. At 9:37 a.m., American Airlines Flight 77 crashed into the Pentagon. At 9:39 a.m., Lauren called me, leaving her sweet message on our answering machine. The passenger manifest showed that Lauren was seated near Honor Elizabeth Wainio, a twenty-seven-year-old Maryland native. Lizz, as she was known to her family, was an all-American girl. At Catonsville High she had been all-county in field hockey, captain of the cheerleading squad, vice president of the Honor Society, and played the viola in the all-county orchestra. Her zest for life was captured by the Henry Miller quote taped to the fridge in her apartment in New Jersey: "The aim of life is to live, and to live means to be aware, joyously, drunkenly, serenely, divinely aware." Lizz brought this spirit to her work with the Discovery Channel Stores and quickly rose to district manager. She was flying to San Francisco for meetings. From aboard United 93, Lizz called home and her stepmom, Esther Heymann, answered. She said a "really nice person" had loaned her a phone; I like to think it was Lauren, and that even at a time like that she was bringing comfort to those around her.

"Elizabeth, I've got my arms around you and I'm holding you and I love you," Esther said, as quoted in the book *Among the Heroes* by Jere Longman.

"I can feel your arms around me," Lizz said, "I love you, too."

As other passengers spoke to their families and learned about the attacks on the Twin Towers and Pentagon, it very quickly became clear that their plane was not going to return to Newark, as the hijackers had initially announced. So, in this harrowing moment they did the most American thing imaginable: they debated and voted on a course of action. It was decided that they would storm the cockpit and try to retake control of the plane. I imagine that Lauren was at the heart of these discussions. Given her boardroom experience and emergency medical technician training, she knew how to use her voice and stay calm under pressure. I can easily picture her tapping her watch and telling the others that it was time to act.

Two passengers offered hope that United 93 could be landed safely: Donald Green had a pilot's license and frequently flew a single-engine seaplane nicknamed "Flying Canoe," while Andrew Garcia had trained as an air traffic controller with the National Guard in California.

An hour earlier, the passengers on United 93 were everyday people just going about their lives. Now they had been thrust into the most extraordinary circumstances imaginable. I still marvel at the courage and calm they displayed in deciding to attempt to disarm the terrorists; two were in the cockpit and two others stationed outside to guard it. Flight attendants began boiling water to use as a weapon. On the phone with his wife, Lyz, Jeremy Glick said, "We just had breakfast and we have our butter knives." It was gallows humor, but Glick, six foot two and 220 pounds, knew how to handle himself; at the University of Rochester, he won a national championship in judo. At 9:57 a.m., Lizz Wainio was still on the phone with her stepmother when she said, "They're getting ready to break into the cockpit. I have to go. I love you. Goodbye." Flight attendant Sandra Bradshaw was also on the phone at that moment with her husband, Phil, a pilot for US Airways. He was at home caring for their two-year-old daughter, Alexandria, and son, Nathan, who was ten days shy of his first birthday. "Everyone is running up to first class," Sandra said. "I've got to go. Bye."

The cockpit recorder captured the ensuing struggle: the sounds of breaking glass and shattering plates, muffled shouting in English and Arabic, screams of pain. Jarrah, the terrorist flying the plane, began pitching it side to side and then up and down, trying to knock the encroaching passengers off balance. A food cart rammed against the cockpit door. As part of their training, the hijackers had been instructed that if their mission was compromised, they were to crash the plane rather than risk losing control of it. In the cockpit, Jarrah asked a coconspirator, "Is that it? Shall we finish it off?"

"No. Not yet. When they all come, we finish it off."

The voice of a male passenger can be heard: "In the cockpit! If we don't, we'll die."

The *9/11 Commission Report* concluded that the hijackers remained in control of the plane and crashed it to thwart the counterattack. Many of the surviving families disagree. I have chosen to never listen to the audio recordings, but those who did listen believe the passengers made it into the cockpit and there was a struggle for the yoke.

At 10:01 a.m., Jarrah asked again, "Is that it? I mean, shall we pull it down?"

"Yes, put it in it, and pull it down."

We'll never know for sure if the passengers made it into the cockpit, but at 10:02 a.m., United 93 plummeted into a nosedive. The yoke was pulled hard to the right, turning the plane upside down. It reached a speed of 575 miles per hour; at 10,000 feet or less the design limit for that plane is 287 miles per hour. Thirty seconds later United 93 crashed into an empty field outside of Shanksville, Pennsylvania.

In the secure bunker beneath the White House, Vice President Dick Cheney had been monitoring the flight path of Lauren's plane. When word came that it had gone down, Cheney said, "I think an act of heroism just took place on that plane."

Indeed, United 93 was the first victory in the battle against terrorism. The passengers gave their lives so others could live. The hijackers were piloting the plane toward either the White House or, more likely, the Capitol Building. With their brave actions, Lauren and the passengers saved countless lives and a powerful iconography of our democracy. A few hours earlier, they had boarded the plane as strangers heading their separate ways. Now their memory will live on together forever, not as victims but as heroes.

4

IN THE DAYS AFTER 9/11, the nation was still coming to grips
with the magnitude of the tragedy. The firefighters who charged
into the crumbling towers, the executives and custodians who
made the awful choice to leap from the buildings to escape the
searing heat, the flyers that had papered Lower Manhattan as
friends and family desperately searched for missing loved ones,
the flames rising from the Pentagon, the doomed uprising on
United 93…it was overwhelming to absorb all the wrenching
stories and images of heartbreak and heroism. The last thing
anyone wanted to do was get on an airplane, but the families of
United 93 passengers were invited by the federal government
to Shanksville to view the crash site and provide information to
investigators. Despite my anxiety about flying, I did feel a strong
pull to see Lauren's final resting place, and I hoped it would
bring a little closure. So, I boarded a United Airlines plane in
San Francisco on the first day that commercial flights resumed.
The security lines were the longest I had ever seen, and you
could read the tension on every face. We were all getting the
first taste of how much 9/11 would alter everyday life.

The United 93 families gathered at the Pittsburgh airport,
waiting for the buses that would take us on the two-hour drive

southeast to Shanksville. Needing all the support I could get, I brought along my mom, sister Soozie, and brother Mark. Lauren's parents met us there. It was eerie to look around at the other clusters of families. We were all in the same zombie state, trying to function but not really living. Soozie still recalls vividly the distress of Lauren's mother. "There were times she was having trouble walking," she says. "I've never seen someone in such shock."

It was a quiet bus ride to Shanksville. I was struck by the pastoral beauty of the countryside. Everything around me felt illuminated to the hundredth degree. I noticed colors and flowers and smells. I noticed things that in the past would have whooshed right by. I recall being fascinated that I was so acutely aware of every single little detail. Something had shifted inside of me, but I didn't know what. For most of the journey it was just empty land, but as we got closer to town the road was suddenly crowded. Lining both sides were police officers, state troopers, and other emergency personnel standing at attention and saluting as we drove by—it seemed like miles and miles of people. What a powerful scene. As we went through town, it seemed like the whole community had turned out to greet us, waving American flags and holding signs, some clapping, some standing with their hand over their heart. We could all feel their love and sorrow. I had spent the previous couple of days holed up in my house, so this was my first time seeing the effect 9/11 had on ordinary Americans. Their support meant so much that my mom talked about these gestures for many years afterward.

The crash site was crowded with investigators and their equipment, all of it ringed by a tall fence. It was still being treated as a crime scene. As soon as we arrived, all the workers in their hazmat suits vacated the area as a showing of respect.

I had already seen many images of that smoking crater—it felt surreal to be standing on a hill near the edge, peering into its abyss. The fence around the perimeter had become a makeshift memorial, covered with American flags, flowers, cards, notes, photos, medals, and a vast array of other mementos. Members of the Shanksville Volunteer Fire Department had signed and hung one of their coats; they were the first emergency unit to arrive at the crash site. A large wooden cross had also been erected. In my pocket were a few photos of Lauren, so I left one there of the two of us, inscribing it, "I'm here. I love you." I didn't know what else to say.

When emergency personnel first arrived at the crash site on 9/11, their initial emotion was confusion: Where was the plane? United 93 had plummeted into a reclaimed mining strip. The plane burrowed into the porous limestone at a forty-five-degree angle, some parts driven thirty feet into the earth. At the speed it was traveling and loaded with more than 11,000 gallons of fuel for the cross-country flight, much of plane disintegrated upon impact and in the ensuing inferno. Among the first investigators on the scene was Somerset County coroner Wallace Miller. He scoured the crash site hoping to rescue survivors, but instead saw no signs of the passengers. They had essentially been cremated upon impact. "If you didn't know, you would have thought no one was on the plane," Miller told author Jere Longman. "You would have thought they dropped them off somewhere." Some 150 FBI officials would spend weeks scouring the crash site on their hands and knees, using sifters to sort through the dirt in hopes of finding any human remains that could be used for identification purposes.

DNA samples were needed to help this process. I had brought along a plastic bag with Lauren's toothbrush and hairs pulled from a brush in our bathroom. After arriving in Shanksville, I had a debriefing with Miller. Lauren's parents joined me. It was pretty intense because FBI agents were on hand, still trying to piece together the sequence of events aboard the plane. I felt so lucky to have Wally Miller on the case. He had enjoyed a pretty quiet life until United 93 fell from the sky. But Wally took on this incredibly difficult job with grace, humility, and respect.

Lauren's wallet with her driver's license had been recovered. It reeked of airplane fuel, which was really eerie. A year later, I received a letter from Dr. Warren Tewes, the member of the Disaster Mortuary Operations Response Team who found Lauren's personal affects. "The operation had just begun when Lauren energized me…probably forever," he wrote. "This moment was not routine. Actually, it was only three or four seconds, but time seemed to stop. Driver's license photographs are rarely flattering but Lauren gave me a look from her picture that was more than inspiring. With a little bit of an attitude, the message I got from her nearly three-dimensional expression was, 'You know me. Now you've got a big job to do for me and the rest of us here. Quit staring and get going.'"

During our stay in Shanksville, the families were put up at a ski resort that had been hastily reopened to accommodate us. It was big and mostly empty, and that just added to the unsettled feeling I'd had ever since arriving. But in the downtime, I did begin to connect with some of the other survivors, including Daniel Belardinelli, whose uncle Bill Cashman was on United 93. I also befriended two women who also hailed from Northern California: Dorothy Garcia, who lost her husband, Andrew, the businessman who had once been an air traffic controller; and Kimi Beaven, who was mourning the loss of her husband, Alan, the environmental lawyer. Their presence brought a little bit of comfort, knowing that someone else could understand the jumble of emotions. We had a few quiet conversations about how each of us was sorting through the mix of grief, anger, and confusion.

The good people of Pennsylvania did their best to recognize those aboard United 93. On one of our first nights there, a sunset memorial service was held in the nearby town of Somerset, every inch of which was decorated with American flags. More than a thousand people ringed the county courthouse. A bell tolled for each of the forty passengers and crew members, and a candle was lit for each victim. Many in the crowd also held lit candles. Governor Tom Ridge hailed all of those aboard United 93, saying, "They sacrificed themselves for others—the ultimate sacrifice." The story of the passengers and crew fighting to reclaim their plane had already become a part of American lore. In some of our nation's darkest hours, it offered a beacon of hope and courage. Ridge made the point that the hijackers had failed in their mission. "They did not destroy our spirit, they rekindled it," he said. "They did not destroy our patriotism. They did not—and we will not let them—take away our way of life." He added, "What appears to be a charred, smoldering hole in the ground is truly and really a monument to heroism."

A more private ceremony was held just for the families, on a bluff above the crash site. Many of us brought flowers, cards, photos, and other items to leave behind. There were a lot of prayers and even more tears. I appreciated getting to know the other surviving families and felt a little bit of strength from their collective presence, but I was utterly exhausted. The whole time we were in Shanksville I was plagued by nightmares. I was holding in a lot of the grief and sorrow during the day, trying to be strong for my mom and siblings. But alone in the dark, the awfulness of the tragedy invaded my dreams. As I was learning, there was no escaping my new reality, even when I closed my eyes.

5

ADRENALINE GOT ME THROUGH the trip to Shanksville, Lauren's funeral in Houston, and the celebration of life in our hometown of San Rafael eleven days after 9/11. When all of that stopped, I was left to rattle around the house, which suddenly felt so empty. I wasn't the only one missing Lauren: our cat, Nicholas, stared out the bay window for hours at a time, hoping his soulmate would finally come home. Knowing that I didn't cook much, my neighbors pitched in and bought me a generous gift certificate to a meal delivery service, so I had no need to ever leave the house.

Within days of the attacks, something unexpected happened: cards and letters began pouring in through the mail. They came from old acquaintances and colleagues but mostly from strangers who just felt compelled to reach out. (I'm not sure how so many folks found my address, but they did.) Along with the kind words came rosaries, Bibles, poems, teddy bears, newspaper clippings, drawings done by school kids in crayon, and much more. I tried to send a personal reply to each, though I could never quite keep up. I was deeply grateful for the support, and writing my replies helped me pass the time—sometimes the days felt endless.

Not long after 9/11, I sat in my living room and watched President Bush's address to Congress, during which he laid out a detailed case that the Al-Qaeda terrorist network led by Osama bin Laden had carried out the attacks. We had already learned much about the hijackers of United 93. Seeing their names and faces didn't fill me with rage, as I would have expected. I couldn't bring myself to hate them because hatred is exactly what fueled their attacks. I almost felt pity for these young men, that their empty lives were so devoid of meaning that they could so easily be led astray. Derrill Bodley lost his daughter Deora on United 93 and, in his grief, he felt compelled to visit Afghanistan to try to understand more about this breeding ground of terror. He was struck by hardships faced by everyday people there, and afterward devoted much of his time and money to doing relief work in Afghanistan. For Derrill, the answer to violence wasn't more violence but rather to uplift the country where the plot was hatched that ultimately took his daughter. If the people there had hope for a better life, then terrorism would no longer be an attractive option. That humanist perspective hit home with me, too.

Watching President Bush's speech to Congress stirred conflicting emotions. I was grateful for the empathy and dignity he displayed in the wake of the attacks—he set the emotional tone for the whole country as we all continued to grieve. But our commander in chief and his administration had failed to protect America from the gathering storm of Al-Qaeda, which had been responsible for a reign of terror stretching back nearly a decade: the 1993 bombing of the World Trade Center; the 1993 ambush and killing of eighteen Army Rangers in Somalia; the 1995 car bombing at a military installation in Riyadh, Saudi Arabia, which left five American soldiers dead; the 1998 bombing of the US embassies in Tanzania and Kenya; and the 2000 assault on the USS *Cole,* which took the lives of seventeen American sailors. Unless you were directly affected, it was easy to ignore the complicated questions of why these attacks were happening. On the day that Lauren, our unborn child, and so many others died, I was befuddled as to who was attacking us and why. It seemed like an unprovoked onslaught that came completely out of the blue. Like virtually every other American, I didn't understand that 9/11 had been two decades in the making, stretching back to when our own government armed Osama bin Laden's private army to help thwart the Soviet incursion into Afghanistan. But the intelligence services knew better. As far back as 1998, President Clinton was given a classified memo entitled "Bin Laden Preparing to Hijack US Aircraft and Other Attacks." In July 2001, an FBI agent wrote an internal memo about Middle Eastern men training at flight schools around Phoenix, speculating they could be connected to Al-Qaeda. (In fact, the man who flew American Airlines Flight 77 into the Pentagon, Hani Hanjour, attended a flight school in Mesa, Arizona.) Five weeks before 9/11, Bush received an intelligence briefing titled "Bin Laden Determined to Strike in US." The *9/11 Commission Report* would lay out a damning case of the government's ineffectual response to all of these warning signs: "The domestic agencies never mobilized in response to the threat. They did not have direction and did not have a plan to institute. The borders were not hardened. Transportation systems were not fortified. Electronic surveillance was not targeted against a domestic threat. State and local law enforcement were not marshaled to augment the FBI's efforts. The public was not warned. The terrorists exploited deep institutional failings within our government." The 9/11 attacks were so cunningly evil perhaps there was no way they could have been thwarted.

But part of me felt like Bush was co-opting the memory of United 93 to deflect blame from the failings of the government and its intelligence agencies.

In attendance at the president's speech to Congress was Lisa Beamer, whose husband, Todd, was one of the passengers. He dialed the operator on a GTE-Verizon airphone to report the hijacking and was patched through to a customer service agent named Lisa Jefferson. Their thirteen-minute call became an important record of the events unfolding on the plane. Together they recited the Lord's Prayer and Psalm 23. (*Though I walk through the valley of the shadow of death, I will fear no evil: for thou art with me; thy rod and thy staff they comfort me.*) As the uprising against the hijackers was about to begin, Todd turned to another passenger and said, "Are you ready? Okay, let's roll." That last bit quickly became a rallying cry in the new War on Terror.

Bush began his speech to Congress by saying, "In the normal course of events, presidents come to this chamber to report on the state of the union. Tonight, no such report is needed. It has already been delivered by the American people. We have seen it in the courage of passengers who rushed terrorists to save others on the ground—passengers like an exceptional man named Todd Beamer. Please help me to welcome his wife, Lisa Beamer, here tonight." Legislators from both sides of the aisle rose to give Lisa a rousing ovation. It was gratifying that the people aboard United 93 received such recognition, and I was pleased for Lisa and especially for her young sons to hear their father celebrated so publicly. But already I was becoming sensitive to the exploitation of the heroes aboard that plane.

Still, when the president summons you, there is an obligation to go. My mom actually answered the first phone call.

46

The person on the line said they were calling from the White House. She was a bit confused and thought it was a neighbor, saying, "Which house are you talking about? I can't see a white house on this block." Eventually we got that straightened out, and on September 24, all of the United 93 families were welcomed by George and Laura Bush. Each of us was given a private audience with the president and First Lady, and they were very gracious hosts. We were also taken to a hallway in the East Wing that was lined on both sides by White House staffers. With United 93 hurtling toward Washington, DC, they had been in grave danger. All of these public servants expressed their heartfelt gratitude for the sacrifice of our loved ones.

A few days after I returned from Washington, I was speaking with other family members and they voiced a troubling feeling that had also been welling up inside of me: it seemed like only four men were being credited with taking action to stop the hijackers when the phone calls home and other emerging evidence already made clear that all of the passengers and crew were a party to the uprising.

Given all the empty seats, it was a quirk of fate that United 93 had on board a handful of big, athletic men who had the disposition to take on the terrorists. There was Jeremy Glick, the high school wrestler and NCAA judo champion; Tom Burnett, who had been a standout high school quarterback who later went through Air Force boot camp; Todd Beamer who played baseball and basketball at Wheaton College in Illinois; and Mark Bingham, a buffed six foot five, who had won two national championships in rugby at Cal and once disarmed a mugger wielding a handgun. Based on all the phone calls made from the plane, it seems likely these four men were part of the group that stormed the cockpit. But others could have been involved, too. Kimi Beaven is convinced she heard her husband's voice on the cockpit recording. Richard Guadagno was the manager of the Humboldt Bay National Wildlife Refuge in Eureka, California. As a federal law enforcement officer, he received the same extensive training as DEA or ATF agents, including in hand-to-hand combat. The night before the flight, Richard was in New Jersey celebrating his grandmother's hundredth birthday. An avid gardener and outdoorsman, he had grabbed a small pickax from the garage and put it in his carry-on bag. It's hard to imagine he wouldn't have been in the middle of any confrontation with the terrorists. Same with Louis Nacke, an avid weightlifter who loved to show off his Superman tattoo. We can't know, and never will, what each person aboard the plane did or didn't do. But they all played a role in the heroism, beginning with the democratic vote to take action. The female flight attendants who thought to boil water to use as a weapon displayed as much cool under pressure as any of the brawny men. Some of the passengers never left their seats during the uprising but they could have given courage to those who did with a poignant word or clasp of the hand. My bride was such a fighter at heart I can easily imagine her giving a pep talk to the guys when it was time to strike. I will forever be grateful for the bravery of Beamer, Bingham, Burnett, and Glick, and for the bravery of all those aboard, who did everything they could under harrowing circumstances. But as the story of United 93 began to be told widely, the focus seemed to narrow to only those four men.

One example came in the September 23 issue of *Sports Illustrated*, at that time one of the most widely read magazines in the country. The back page column by Rick Reilly carried the headline "Four of a Kind." Reilly wrote, "Beamer, Bingham,

Burnett, and Glick must have realized their jet was a guided missile. The four apparently came up with a plan." In the darkness after 9/11 this country needed points of light. I understand it was easier for the media to focus on a few individuals rather than a plane full of them, but it was the collective action of all the passengers that made United 93's journey so quintessentially American. It didn't feel right for any of them to be excluded. Reilly also wrote, "In Washington, a movement grew in Congress to give the four men the Presidential Medal of Freedom, the highest award a civilian can receive." In fact, when Congressional Gold Medals were later awarded, all forty of the passengers and crew were recognized, as it should be.

It was stories like Reilly's and others that compelled Coach to call me. To that point, I had ignored countless media requests. But Coach and I had a heart-to-heart and I agreed that Lauren needed a voice, so I consented to a handful of TV interviews. I didn't speculate on the actions of anyone else aboard the plane, I just told the public what a special person Lauren was and that her bravery was evident by her message to me. It was bittersweet talking about her, and there were times when I struggled to hold it together.

I did use each interview as a chance to thank all those who had sent me notes and to apologize for not personally responding. Boy did that backfire, because after that I got more mail than ever. Mrs. Andrea Bildstein from Solon, Iowa, sent me a package of handmade cards from her seventh-grade social studies class. A girl named Emily decorated hers with pink and red hearts. On the inside she wrote only two sentences: "I'm sorry. It must be so hard without her." You can't read something like that and not have your heart break a little more.

But there was a lot of wisdom in the letters, too. One that really helped came from Ray Gaulke, my old boss at *USA Weekend*. He wrote, "It's so hard to find the right words but what I've learned through sailing is that the only way through a storm is to meet it head on." That really resonated because I knew there were rough waters ahead.

6

I LOST THIRTY POUNDS in the three months after 9/11. I thought I had cancer. When I went to see my doctor, he actually laughed at the suggestion. "You don't have cancer, Jack," he said. "You're suffering from depression."

With my traditional Midwestern upbringing, I must admit that I always felt a stigma around depression. I didn't know what an insidious disease it was. Among the side effects is a suppressed appetite, which explained my weight loss. My doctor urged me to see a therapist. I followed his advice, despite my misgivings, and it turned out to be one of the best decisions of my life. The way I lost Lauren was unique, but everyone has tragedies in their life, whether from cancer or a car accident. The sadness and anger and confusion can be overwhelming. What I learned is that you need help to find your way through the darkness.

Twice a week I saw my therapist, an older gentleman with kind eyes and a soft voice. With him I didn't have to pretend to be strong, or that everything was okay. That alone relieved some of my burden. He also provided some direction to help me carry on. The first step was to take care of unfinished business. By facing the things I was hiding from, it would allow me to look forward instead of backward. I hadn't touched a thing in the house since 9/11. Lauren's possessions were exactly as she left them, which brought me comfort. I would still go into the closet and smell her clothes, and many of the shirts, sweaters, or dresses triggered a specific memory of where and when she had worn them. I know I wasn't alone among the widowers and widows of United 93 in that need to hang on to something tangible: for months after the crash Liz Glick called her husband's cell phone, just to hear Jeremy's voice, while Lorne Lyles sprayed his wife, CeeCee's, perfume on a teddy bear and slept next to it in bed. (CeeCee was one of the flight attendants on the plane. A onetime police officer, she also left behind four sons.) After long talks with my therapist, I knew it was time to start letting go, so I packed up most of Lauren's clothes. A few things went to her sisters, but the rest was donated to a shelter in San Rafael for women fleeing abusive relationships that Lauren had long supported. It made me feel good to know that her stylish clothes would be providing a small bit of solace for those in need.

I tried to keep pushing myself beyond my comfort zone. This Midwestern boy tried acupuncture and meditation, and I found that each brought me a little more peace. I often came back to something my therapist told me: "You need to have pace and balance. It's like riding a bike—you can't go too slow or too fast." To this day I still use that simple thought...*pace and balance.*

This became even more important as I tried to reintegrate into my old life, beginning with a gradual return to work. Before, I had enjoyed many different identities: executive vice president, enthusiastic golfer, native Hoosier, Texas grad, adoring husband. Now I was defined by only one thing—I was the guy who lost his wife on 9/11. No one quite knew what to say to me, and I was still learning how to navigate the interactions, too. Just the look in people's eye or the tone of their voice made me recoil. I came to dread all the small talk. Six months after 9/11, I attended a large conference to let my clients know I was still standing. Many had come to the celebration of Lauren's life in San Rafael, and others had made special trips just to take me out to lunch or dinner, but contact had been infrequent, and I thought it was important to show up at such a visible event. Arriving for the luncheon at a fancy LA hotel, the valet attendant ran over my foot and nearly knocked me down with the side-view mirror as he sped by. The hotel management polished the tire tracks off my patent leather shoe and insisted I go to the hospital for X-rays. I returned to the luncheon on crutches…not exactly the low-key entrance I was seeking. At least that gave everyone else an easy icebreaker.

There were many days when I didn't want to leave the house to go to work. But Lauren kept me going. Her presence remained powerful, and there were times when I could hear her voice in my head: *Hey, don't let them get you, too. I want you to fight on in my spirit.* Some days I'd lay in bed and say out loud, "I can't do this. I can't get up." And I could feel Lauren telling me, *You can do it, and I will help.* It was just like fifteen years earlier when I got my big break with *USA Weekend* and she pushed me to nail my interview despite having an injured ankle. Once again she was my strength, helping me through this. I don't bring this up lightly, but her spirit was there for me in a very real way. *Get out of bed. Go eat some breakfast. One foot in front of the other. Breathe.* She was telling me how to live, how to survive. Lauren's favorite movie was *The Shawshank Redemption* and the line she loved the most was when the character Andy Dufresne says, "I guess it comes down to a simple choice, really: get busy livin' or get busy dyin'." I was trying my hardest to live. Another line from the movie resonated: "Hope is a good thing, maybe the best of things. And no good thing ever dies."

There were setbacks, of course. One day in April 2002—the month that our baby would have arrived—I caught a glimpse of Ari Fleischer on the TV news. The White House press secretary under President Bush was saying that the government never imagined terrorists would use airplanes as weapons. *Really*? That had been happening going back to World War II kamikazes. What about the small plane that crashed onto the White House lawn in 1994? That had been an ordinary mechanical failure, but the wayward plane could have taken out much of the White House. What about the 2000 meeting between the federal Counterterrorism Security Group examining the possibility that the crash of EgyptAir Flight 990, off the coast of Massachusetts, had been the result of an Al-Qaeda hijacking plot? Or the FBI agent who in the months before 9/11 had warned of possible Al-Qaeda members taking classes at flight schools around Phoenix? Hearing Fleischer's empty words made me feel like I was being lied to and that the American people were not getting the whole truth. I felt like I wanted to throw up. I yelled at the TV. I shouted at the heavens. For a few days after that I went to a very dark place.

But in the bleakness there were always a couple rays of sunshine: Kimi Beaven and Dorothy Garcia. Each lost her husband on United 93. I had gotten to know them a little bit on the trip to Shanksville and in the months afterward they became a big part of my life. I would talk by phone to one or both of them nearly every day. The calls could last for hours. They helped break up the isolation and loneliness. We were all grappling with shock, denial, and stress, and in that state it's easy for the mind to do strange things. I'd say, "I can't stop thinking this—am I going crazy?" And Dorothy or Kimi would invariably say, "I was feeling exactly the same way." That was always a relief. We would take turns cheering each other up, and that felt good, too. I had always been there to provide emotional support for Lauren, and there was a warm familiarity in playing that role for Kimi and Dorothy, as they did for me.

That first holiday season was particularly tough. Lauren loved to put up a big Christmas tree and fill our home with cheer. I couldn't muster the energy for any of that, so the house was quiet and barren. One day in mid-December, I was on the phone with Kimi, feeling particularly morose. She said that we both needed to get out of the house. I mentioned that I had an invitation to a Christmas party that night but didn't really want to go, and certainly not alone. Kimi perked up when she heard that. "That's it, we're going to the party," she said. "I'm getting in my car and driving over to your house and you can't stop me." And that's exactly what she did. After so many hours on the phone, it was the first time we had seen each other since the trip to Shanksville. What a hug that was.

The party was at the house of Nick Graham, the Joe Boxer founder who had been so impressed with Lauren when he brought his business to PricewaterhouseCoopers. He lived one town over from me in Kentfield. There were maybe three dozen people there, and it was a pretty sparkly crowd, including Lars Ulrich from Metallica and Jerry Harrison from Talking Heads. In my old life I would have been a little starstruck and eager to mingle with these famous musicians. Now, I couldn't have cared less. Kimi and I hid out on the patio, keeping to ourselves. We were huddled in conversation when the actor and director Sean Penn strolled up, asking if either of us had a light.

(Back then he and his wife, Robin Wright, and their children lived in the nearby town of Ross.) I didn't smoke but for some reason I did have a pack of matches in my pocket, so I helped Sean get his cigarette lit. Just making conversation, he asked, "So, how do you guys know Nick?" I let out a big sigh and that's when Kimi put her hand on my chest and said, "I'll take care of this." She told Sean that we had each lost our spouse on United 93. He squinted at us, took a drag of his cigarette, and said, "I've got a hero's poem for ya, would you be okay if I share it?" And then he recited like a poet the lyrics to "Heroes," a song about love and loss by the LA band David & David:

Sean's voice made the song come alive, and its meaning hit Kimi and I quite hard. It was a powerful bonding moment and after that Sean integrated us into the party, making introductions and watching over us. Before long, Kimi was in the middle of the living room, belting out Christmas carols. Seeing her have such a joyous time put a big smile on my face. Sean spent the rest of the night making conversation with me. It turns out he's a very inquisitive, compassionate guy, qualities that would later be on display with his relief work in Haiti and post-Katrina New Orleans as well as his nonprofit CORE, which led the charge to make COVID testing and vaccinations more readily available, particularly in communities of color. I guess Sean could see I was hurting and a bit lost and he felt for me. I didn't care that he was a movie star, it was just nice to have someone with whom to talk about life. Kimi and I stayed at the party until nearly 2:00 a.m. Before we left, Sean and I exchanged phone numbers and he encouraged me to keep in touch. I appreciated the gesture, but doubted I'd ever see him again. Still, I was grateful that Sean helped Kimi and I enjoy a respite for at least one night.

Pace and balance. That was the constant challenge. At the office I resumed tending to my big accounts but felt rudderless. I had always worked so hard for one specific purpose: to provide a nice life for Lauren. She was my motivation, whether it was to pay for our three-month honeymoon across Europe, to buy Lauren her dream home, or to provide a nest egg for our child. Overnight, work lost its meaning.

I also felt consumed tending to the Lauren Catuzzi Grandcolas Foundation. All of her friends and family struggled in the aftermath of 9/11 to make sense of Lauren's death, so the foundation became a way to honor her memory and do some good in the communities she left behind. Lauren's father pushed hard for us to hold a charity golf tournament pegged to the one-year anniversary of 9/11 and it fell to me to manage the many logistical details, which at times felt overwhelming.

I wanted to maintain a close relationship with Lauren's family, but it became complicated. I was already suffering brutal survivor's guilt and abandonment issues. I had spent my entire adult life trying to take care of Lauren and the one time I let her out of my sight the worst thing imaginable happened. I continued to struggle to make sense of the world and my place in it and that extended to Lauren's family. I could feel things changing between Coach and me. We had gone fishing many times and played a lot of golf together. We'd have good battles on the course that featured lots of ribbing. I always felt lucky to have Coach in my life. A strong, level-headed man, he was well liked by all who knew him, and I greatly admired his and Barbara's marriage. In June 2002, I was in New York on business, so I decided to spend Father's Day weekend with Lauren's entire family at her sister's home in New Jersey. The holiday weighed heavily on me, as it should have been my first as a dad. No one else seemed to recognize that pain. I also felt that I was now a reminder of what their family had lost. How could my presence help them? There was no solace in being together, only sadness—for me, too, as their closeness was another reminder of what Lauren and I should have had. I left that weekend with another thing to mourn, knowing that the dynamic with Lauren's family had changed and it would be tough for us to be together moving forward. The collateral damage caused by losing a loved one can have an unexpected effect on all of those left behind.

Still, we pressed on with the charity golf tournament, which was to be held at the Marin Country Club, where I played most of my golf. It provided a glimpse of the true American spirit as so many friends, acquaintances, and strangers made generous donations for the auction or volunteered their time to help pull off the whole thing. Enough money was raised for the foundation to donate $50,000 to the Texas Children's Hospital in Houston, where Lauren had gone to high school. A pair of $4,000 scholarships were given to a couple of exceptional young women graduating high school in economically depressed communities. And $50,000 was donated to create a birthing room at Marin General Hospital, where Lauren had planned to deliver our baby. The birthing room is quite spacious, with a couch that pulls out into a bed if the new father wants to sleep over. All the equipment is on hand, so a woman can give birth right there in the room and not have to be moved afterward. A friend of ours, Kimberly Jones, created an abstract painting of Lauren holding a baby on Mount Tamalpais, a landmark around Marin. It hangs on the wall of the birthing room and my heart always bursts when I see it. The room is a lovely way to honor the memory of Lauren and the child we never got to meet. I once received a letter from a family who delivered their son in Lauren's room and they were so moved by our story they named the boy Jack in my honor, a gesture I found deeply touching. A couple friends have also had their kids there, and they reported that Lauren's presence was palpable. In fact, there's a brass plaque in the room dedicated to her. It reads, *May her courage give us strength and her bravery give us hope.*

There was something so bittersweet in Lauren's death helping others joyously bring life into this world. I felt the same jumble of emotions when it was time to take possession of her ashes. It took many months of DNA analysis for all the remains at the crash site to be identified. Finally, the good folks in Shanksville shipped the ashes to a mortuary near my home. At the appointed time I drove over to pick them up. I placed the dark wooden urn on the passenger seat and buckled it in with the seatbelt. For a while I just sat in the parking lot, taking deep breaths. I felt sorrow, of course, but also a profound relief. Lauren was finally coming home.

7

THERE WAS A LOT of buildup to the first anniversary of 9/11, though I disliked the use of that word; an anniversary should be a time for celebration. This was a day of infamy. I felt a strong pull to be in Shanksville for the ceremonies, which were beautiful but somber. The Second Marine Aircraft Wing band played a series of songs, including a moving rendition of "God Bless America." A local Eagle Scout led the Pledge of Allegiance and then an opera singer performed a rousing version of the national anthem, punctuated by a military flyover that made the hairs on my arm stand up. Sandy Dahl, the widow of pilot Jason Dahl, spoke for all the families that had been left behind. "After September eleventh, we know there is no shortage of angels," she said. "May God bless us."

Another speaker was Murial Borza, age eleven, who lost her sister Deora Bodley in the crash. She asked for a moment of silence, calling it "one minute of peace." She urged all of us to use this time of reflection to "make a pledge to do a good deed or help mankind in some small way, even if it's just a hug, a kiss, a smile, wave, a prayer, or just silent thoughts of someone you love." At exactly 10:03 a.m., the same time as the plane had crashed, a 2,000-pound bell tolled forty times, once for each of the passengers and crew.

All of the United 93 family members were seated together—the first time we had gathered since the White House visit more than eleven months earlier. Now, as we waited for the president and First Lady to place a wreath at the crash site, I looked around at the faces of the family members: Black, white, Asian, Hispanic, young, old. It struck me that the people on the plane represented what's great about America—the diversity of our melting pot and our common purpose. I thought about the 2,977 people who had been killed on 9/11. Each one left behind so many heartbroken loved ones just like us. Sitting at the exact spot where Lauren's life had ended, feeling a whole community—and, indeed, the rest of the nation—mourning along with us, I was overwhelmed by the magnitude of the tragedy. I hadn't cried in a long time but now the tears came again.

Something Pennsylvania Governor Mark Schweiker said at the ceremony stuck with me. Earlier in the day he had visited with schoolchildren in Shanksville, and he repeated a maxim he had picked up in their presence: "If God brought you to it, God will get you through it." Invocations of the almighty had been a constant in the year after 9/11 and, frankly, I was struggling with it.

I had been raised Catholic. While attending elementary school, a particularly stern nun insisted on calling me John, even after my mother brought in my birth certificate to show them I had been baptized as Jack. "John is the Catholic version of Jack," my mom was told by the nun. "There is no St. Jack."

"Not yet there isn't," was Mom's typically tart reply.

One day in second grade, we were discussing St. Nick's imminent arrival on Christmas eve. The nun leading the discussion said he came through the chimney to reward faithful children with goodies. I raised my hand and asked what happened if the house didn't have a fireplace. She said in that case St. Nick would come in through an open window. Since it was winter, I knew the windows of every house would be shut tight. I raised my hand again and asked how St. Nick could get presents through a closed window. "Magically," the nun said, not trying to disguise the irritation in her voice. Well, not long before that, I had smashed a neighbor's window with an errant golf ball, costing me a spanking and four months' allowance, so I knew things couldn't just magically pass through glass. I said as much to the class. I wasn't being a smart aleck, just applying the guileless logic of a little boy. The nun fixed me with a hard stare and then sent the class out to recess. When we came back, the stockings taped to every kid's chair were full of candy and trinkets…except mine, which had only the branch of a tree and a long note that purported to have been written by St. Nick. The nun told the class to be seated and for me to stand and read out loud my note from St. Nick. I was horrified but did as I was told. With my voice cracking, I read, "Chew, John, on this stick and maybe then you will believe I am not fake." I thought the nun was crazy, but I did as instructed, even though I felt bullied and embarrassed. I broke off a little twig, chewed on it and pretended to eat it. That wasn't good enough for her—she insisted I eat the whole branch! When the nun wasn't looking, I threw most of it out of the classroom window. Still, the whole incident was traumatizing. When my mom heard about it, she pulled me out of the school.

Ever since then, religiosity had left me a little befuddled. So, I didn't know how to take it when the events of 9/11 were ascribed to God's will. Lisa Beamer—the widow of Todd, who was pregnant with their third child when United 93 went down—writes in her book *Let's Roll*, "In those days following the crash, this truth became evermore real to me: God knows exactly *what* we need…*when* we need it." In another passage she says, "I have chosen to believe God, to believe he loves me and has a plan for now and eternity. I don't claim to understand, but I choose daily—even moment by moment—to have faith not in what is seen but in what is unseen."

I couldn't share the same blind belief. In some ways, it reminded me of the zealotry of the men who hijacked the planes on 9/11. Incredibly, at the crash site in Shanksville a five-page document was discovered that the hijackers had brought on board, presumed to have been handwritten by Mohamed Atta, the terrorist ringleader. The pages are crowded with references to the almighty and his will. It concludes by saying, "God, I trust in you. God, I lay myself in your hands. There is no God but God…We are of God, and to God we return." Eight seconds before United 93 smashed into the Pennsylvania countryside, the cockpit recorder captured the hijackers shouting, "Allah is the greatest! Allah is the greatest!" I didn't quite understand how both the perpetrators of 9/11 and those whose lives were torn asunder on that day could find the same comfort in their gods.

I wished Lauren could have provided some spiritual guidance for me. She had never been a religious person but, ironically, in the months before 9/11 she had become more curious, attending a weekly Bible study with friends. One evening she came home and said, "I finally get it."

"Get what?"

"The meaning of it all."

I wanted to hear more but she said, "It's too deep to explain, but I want you to know I get it." I wish now that I had pushed her to tell me more, but I didn't. And then she was gone. What kind of merciful God would take my sweet Lauren and our child? It was a vexing question with which I continued to grapple.

∾

I RETURNED HOME FROM Shanksville to a life that remained in transition. Many of my friends were still there for me—I will always be especially grateful to those who were consistent in their love and support. I could mention many but they know who they are. Sadly, as time went by, many of the other couples with whom Lauren and I socialized started to drift away. Maybe they felt awkward that I was now alone, or perhaps it was just her they had liked all along. In any event, I needed a new social circle. Sean Penn, of all people, helped fill the void. After our chance encounter at the Christmas party, he continued to reach out, regularly inviting me for meals or just to hang out at his home. At the time he was married to the actress Robin Wright, who was the sweetest, most welcoming presence, always doting on their kids, Hopper Jack and Dylan. Sean often had a handful of buddies over and we'd gather in the game room above the garage, playing pool, enjoying a beverage or two, and talking about life. Nick Graham was part of the clique. When he was asked why he thinks Sean took me in, Nick said, "September eleventh was such a chaotic, unsettling event. For all Americans, of course, but for those of us on the West Coast there was this powerful feeling of disconnection. We literally slept through it. It happened far away, and we could only experience it through the television. Sean is a guy who craves connection. He wants to experience world events firsthand. If a city is devastated by a hurricane, he's going to get in a boat and start pulling people out of the water. If a country is leveled by an earthquake, he wants to start moving rubble. In Jack, here was a deep connection to

September eleventh, and he could help this person through the simple act of friendship. Sean has a real depth to him, and so does Jack. I think Jack felt he had to be strong for a lot of people, in some sense play a certain role. He could be vulnerable around us, and that's what Sean responds to—authenticity and people just being real."

One day Sean was at my house, and we got on the topic of the surprise skydive Lauren inspired me to participate in for her thirtieth birthday. Sean was intrigued and asked to see the video. I obliged, happily, because it's always been one of my favorite things to watch. The video is seven minutes long, following Lauren from the moment she jumps until she touches down in a field in the wine country north of San Francisco. The videographers incorporated some cool slow-motion shots and they always hit me hard, Lauren with a giant smile on her face, her arms stretched wide, soaring like a bird, or maybe an angel. It was a crystal-clear day and when the camera would point up at the sun, the light would overwhelm the shot in a divine way. I had touched down moments before her, so I couldn't wait to greet Lauren when she landed. I run into the frame like a puppy dog, bouncing around with a goofy grin on my face. Watching that always makes me laugh even as I'm wiping away the tears.

For the background music to the video, Lauren chose U2's "One Tree Hill." It's such a beautiful, spiritual song and it's the perfect soundtrack to the jump. Sean asked about the song's significance, and I told him the whole story about my first night out with Lauren being at a U2 concert and how she didn't know it was a date until I showed up at her door with a bottle of wine and bouquet of flowers. I pulled out my wallet and removed the ticket stub from that show, which I had carried with me every day since. I told Sean that I felt an even deeper connection to

U2 because at one of their concerts in the aftermath of 9/11, they displayed on a screen the names of every person who had been killed in the attacks. A friend of mine happened to be at the concert and sent me a picture of Lauren's name alighting the screen. Sean loved every bit of the story.

In 2005, U2 announced an upcoming concert at the Oakland Coliseum. I was delighted when Sean told me he would get us tickets; I had seen the band perform only once since that first date with Lauren two decades earlier. Sean was friendly with Bono and, unbeknownst to me, he rang him up and shared the whole story of Lauren and I. Sean asked if he would dedicate a song to us at the concert and Bono happily agreed, until he heard it had to be "One Tree Hill."

"I'll do any other song but that one," Bono said.

He explained to Sean that "One Tree Hill" was written for Greg Carroll, a New Zealander of Maori descent. In 1984, while the band was on tour, Bono was roaming around Auckland late at night when he had a chance encounter with Carroll. They wound up making a pilgrimage to a volcanic peak that holds spiritual significance in the Maori culture. Its name is Maungakiekie, which translates to "one tree hill." Carroll became Bono's close friend and was hired as a soundman for the band. In 1986, on a rainy night in Dublin, Carroll died in a crash while riding Bono's motorcycle. The lyrics for "One Tree Hill" came to Bono at Carroll's funeral, as he reflected on their first night together. According to band lore, the song was recorded in only one take, because Bono was too overwrought to sing it twice. It had been more than fifteen years since U2 performed "One Tree Hill" in concert because it remained highly emotional for them.

It will probably come as no surprise to hear that Sean Penn can be utterly relentless. He kept pushing Bono to do "One Tree Hill" for me and Lauren, and Bono kept saying no. Sean made him discuss it with the band and still Bono was resisting. On the night of the concert, Sean didn't know what was going to happen.

A big group of us road tripped to the Coliseum and were given special seats in a small staging area near the technicians operating the lights and mixing boards. When I wasn't around, Sean gathered the crew—which included actor Robin Williams and cyclist Lance Armstrong—and told them, "If Jack wants a beer, give him yours. If he says he's gotta go to the bathroom, let him piss in your cup. We can't let him leave this area for any reason 'cause I don't know when Bono is gonna dedicate the song to Lauren."

U2 put on a great show. For the final encore, the Coliseum went dark and then Bono and The Edge came out with acoustic guitars, under lonely spotlights. Bono walked to the microphone, bowed his head and said, "This song is for beautiful Lauren." A jolt of electricity ran through my body. I looked at Sean and asked, "Did he just say what I think he said?" He just gave me a wily smile but didn't utter a word. I knew right then something big was happening. With deep feeling in his voice, Bono began singing "One Tree Hill":

We turn away to face the cold, enduring chill/
As the day begs the night for mercy, love/
A sun so bright it leaves no shadows/
Only scars carved into stone on the face of earth/
The moon is up and over One Tree Hill/
We see the sun go down in your eyes

When he got to the chorus, he changed the prepositions in honor of Lauren:

She runs like a river on to the sea/
She runs like a river to the sea.

Bono was unable to go on. "God bless you, Lauren," he said, ending the song early. It was surreal. It was beautiful and magical. "The whole night had a mythical quality to it," said my friend John McGleenan, a sound engineer who grew up in Ireland. "If you know the band and the history of that song, you knew you were witnessing a once-in-a-lifetime moment."

As soon as Bono was done singing, I buried my face in my hands and at that moment I felt hugs coming from both sides of me. When I looked up, it was the unbelievable sight of being smooshed between Robin Williams and Lance Armstrong. Sean looked at me and said, "You okay?"

I really was not. I was so overwhelmed I said, "I think I need a moment alone in the bathroom," and then I bolted. Sean sent a couple of close friends after me to make sure I was all right. They found me leaning against a wall, steadying myself. I assured them that these were happy tears. Then I said, "I really have to pee. Do you guys mind?"

The night was far from over. We were invited to the band's after-party and became part of a police-led caravan from Oakland into San Francisco, ultimately being ushered into a big room on the top floor of the Four Seasons. Right away Sean gave a toast to the band and then brought Bono over to me. He was so warm and kind. I told him that the lyrics to his songs had taken on different meanings for me since Lauren's death. I quoted a riff from the song "Walk On": "*You're packing a suitcase for a place none of us has been/A place that has to be believed to be seen.*"

Bono took off his blue-tinted sunglasses and looked deep into my eyes. "Oh, you get that now, do you?" he asked.

"Don't worry, you'll get to see Lauren again." I wanted so badly to believe him, but I couldn't feel it in my heart.

I told Bono, "You're a very religious man and you have belief. I was brought up Catholic, but I don't practice anymore. I've had some experiences that renew my faith, but I still struggle. Being brought up Catholic, you're given all this guilt about things that you didn't do right. I worry that I may have screwed up in this life and mortgaged my opportunity to see Lauren again."

Bono put his hand on my shoulder and said, "You'll see her again. You'll see her again. I know it. We all screw up in life."

"But I've screwed up plenty of times."

"We all screw up, Jack. I screwed up just four days ago. That's why God grants us forgiveness. It's his most powerful gift."

Those words hit me hard. In that moment I felt unburdened. Ever since 9/11, I had questioned God and his plan for me. What Bono said finally gave me new hope, and a profound belief that I would get to see Lauren again on the other side. The night was a tribute to her but in a very important way it set me free, allowing me to be more forgiving of myself and rekindle my belief in God's mercy.

Bono brought up the underlying meaning of "One Tree Hill": "The river is the journey we are all on, the sea is the afterlife. It's where we all meet again. I think there's a reason why your Lauren loved that song so much."

At that point, Sean interrupted the conversation to ask, "Did you show him the ticket stub?"

I had been too embarrassed to say anything but Bono wanted to see it. I fished the stub out of my wallet, and he studied it carefully, including the date: February 26, 1985. "We were a baby band," he said wistfully. Then Bono noticed the price of the ticket. "$12.50!?" he said. "We weren't worth shit, were we?"

"Lauren loved you at that concert," I said to Bono. "She spent the whole night virtually ignoring me and staring at you. She only married me because she couldn't have you."

He giggled and then asked, "May I sign it?" Bono sat down in a nearby chair. In careful script, he wrote, *Like a river to the sea, Lauren.* Then he turned it over. *See you for a swim, Bono.*

8

FROM THE MOMENT I stared down the FBI agents on 9/11, I knew instinctively that I needed to protect Lauren's voicemail. Her lovely words meant everything to me, so on the advice of John McGleenan I copyrighted the recording. I had no interest in profiteering, but it was very important to be able to assert control of where and how her voice message would be used. Lauren's parents made it clear that they did not want to hear the recording, so that weighed heavily on me; my worst fear was that they would be watching TV one day and suddenly be confronted by their daughter's final words without any warning. I turned down many, many requests to use the recording in news programs and made-for-TV movies.

At the same time, I understood that 9/11 is bigger than me and even bigger than Lauren. Thanks to the smattering of interviews I had done, the context of her message had already become part of the narrative, a record of not only what transpired aboard United 93, but also a monument to the human capacity to love unconditionally even when facing death. It was inevitable that Lauren's final message would inspire people, including those moved to tell the story of 9/11. There is a line in the Broadway musical *Rent* that speaks to this: "The opposite of war is not peace, it's creation." Art would play an important role in helping all of us process the events of 9/11 and their larger meaning.

In the months after United 93 crashed, I received a handwritten, heartfelt letter from the Mexican director Alejandro González Iñárritu, who had received much critical acclaim for his movies *Amores Perros* and *Babel*. (He would later win the Oscar for Best Director for both *Birdman* and *The Revenant*.) Alejandro was one of eleven directors contributing a nine-minute-and-eleven-second short film for *11 September*, the release of which was pegged to the first anniversary of the attacks. The directors came from eleven different countries, including unexpected places like Burkina Faso and Bosnia-Herzegovina. (Sean Penn was chosen to be the American director.) Alejandro wanted to use Lauren's voicemail in his short film. I was touched by the letter, and after meeting him for lunch I had no doubt that Alejandro's heart was in the right place, so I gave him my blessing.

11 September is a powerful film, full of grace notes. The opening short is set in Iran, featuring children who toil to make bricks out of mud. The girls wear hijabs, as does their teacher in a makeshift classroom at the brick factory. All of the dialogue is in Farsi with no subtitles. The inquisitive faces of the kids and the passion of their teacher is a statement of universal humanity.

Alejandro's contribution begins with a black screen. Distorted human voices are heard, finally clarifying into news reports about the planes hitting the Twin Towers. The reports grow more urgent and frenzied. Brief flashes interrupt the blackness on the screen, showing images of the plummeting people who jumped from the towers to escape the searing heat. Sirens and screaming can be heard. Then the sounds soften.

A handful of voicemails play, from desperate people reaching out to their loved ones. Lauren's is one of them, slightly condensed for the movie: "*Honey, are you there? Jack? Pick up, sweetie. Okay, well, I just want to tell you I love you. We're having a little problem on the plane…I just love you more than anything, just know that. It's just a little problem, so…Honey, I just love you. Please tell my family I love them, too. Bye, honey.*" The background noise intensifies and then there is footage of the towers collapsing. The screen goes black and for nearly a minute a somber piece of chamber music by the Kronos Quartet plays. Words appear, first in Sanskrit and then English: *Does God's light guide us or blind us?* The words disappear in a bright flash, and the short film ends. It is incredibly difficult to watch but the message has always stuck with me: those consumed by hate are blinded by the light, but that same luminescence can be a beacon that leads down a different, more loving path.

11 September is a unique and moving collection of short films, but the movie is hardly mainstream. It was inevitable that the dramatic events of that day would get a more traditional Hollywood treatment. The horrors around the Twin Towers had been intensely visual, as Alejandro reminded us in his short film. A common refrain about footage of United 175 slamming into the South Tower, and the subsequent collapse of both buildings, was that it looked like a movie. So, I wasn't surprised when the first big film about 9/11 was centered on United 93, not the Twin Towers. Because no footage existed of the crash or the events aboard the plane that preceded it, a movie about United 93 promised to be deeply dramatic.

In the days and months after 9/11, the United 93 families had grown accustomed to communicating through group emails. There was an understanding that we would collectively discuss any proposals that impacted us, whether it was a prospective movie or the monument slowly taking shape in Shanksville. When we were approached in late 2004 by the director Paul Greengrass about making a movie based on United 93, I was asked by a few from the group to vet him. I talked to Sean Penn, who said, "An angel must be looking out for all of you because he is the perfect guy."

Greengrass grew up in England and got his start as a director for ITV, a national public television network. His cinematic work mixed journalism and storytelling, notably his 2002 movie *Bloody Sunday,* which told the story of the 1972 killing of political protestors in Northern Ireland by British soldiers. (This tragic day also informs the work of U2.) For his movie about United 93, Greengrass had the backing of major players like Universal Pictures and StudioCanal. (His profile as a director had risen dramatically with the 2004 release of *The Bourne Supremacy*, the successful second installment in the Jason Bourne franchise.) But Greengrass knew it was vital to have the support and cooperation of the families, so he held meetings in San Francisco and New York to introduce himself to as many of us as possible.

I attended the San Francisco gathering, in a conference room at one of the big hotels near the airport. There were about fifteen of us on hand and the atmosphere was tense. Who gets to decide the memory of your loved ones? It is a fraught question. Certain families had already become accustomed to their son or husband being celebrated as one of the United 93 heroes and wanted assurances that would continue. Other families shared the frustration that many of the other people aboard had never been given their proper due for whatever role they had played in the uprising. At one point, we had to take a break and step outside the room because the tension became a little too intense for some. But Paul Greengrass is an eloquent guy with an unflappable presence, and he skillfully managed all the emotion in the room. He promised to tell the story as truthfully and accurately as possible; however, Greengrass did make it clear that it was his movie and once filmmaking commenced, he would not be entertaining editorial suggestions from forty families. During the meeting, he asked for our feedback and one of the widows voiced a common concern: *Is it too soon?* That's when I spoke up. I said that more than three years had already passed, and it would take another year or two to make and distribute the film—what would it accomplish to wait any longer? We had already lived through 9/11, surely we were strong enough to handle the release of a movie. I told the group that it was inevitable that United 93 would be dramatized and we were lucky to have a caring, conscientious director at the helm. In the end, all the families supported Greengrass and the movie, entitled *United 93,* was a go.

The public premiere came at the Tribeca Film Festival in April 2006, but the families were given preview screenings ahead of that. Two dozen of us gathered at a movie theater in San Francisco. Greengrass was in Europe at the time, but through a live video link he welcomed us and introduced the film. There was a palpable energy in that theater. I had a pit in my stomach from the opening minutes. The movie plays out almost like a documentary, beginning with the banalities of preparing the airplane and the everyday chit-chat of the crew and passengers as they settle into their routines. This is interspersed with images of the hijackers going through their morning preparations: praying, shaving, packing their carry-ons. Their grim determination is a stark contrast to the sleepy-eyed friendliness of the passengers.

With a jarring suddenness, the events of 9/11 unfold as planes begin straying off course. The jocularity of the various air traffic control centers gives way to confusion and then panic. The utter unpreparedness of our civil and military defense systems is laid bare. Aboard United 93, the hijacking finally unfolds. You know it's coming but the savagery of the knife-wielding terrorists is still shocking. The mood of the passengers slowly evolves from fear to determination, though Greengrass is unsparing in portraying the raw emotion as they all grapple with the awful gravity of the situation. The rebellion to take back the plane is both satisfying and melancholy; there is a deep pride in the bravery of the passengers but, seeing the struggle come to life, you realize what a long shot it was to succeed. In depicting the plane's final moments, Greengrass sided with family members' interpretation of the audio recordings and not the analysis of the 9/11 Commission, so the passengers do make it into the cockpit. Up until that moment, the terrorist flying the plane, Ziad Jarrah, had been depicted as unsteady and perhaps even conflicted in his mission. But in the frenzied battle in the cockpit, Jarrah fights hard to pull down the yoke, sending the plane plummeting to the earth. The screen goes dark just before impact.

It was very quiet when the movie ended. We were all wrung out. I slumped in my chair, trying to process what had been a harrowing 110 minutes. My emotions were mixed over Lauren's portrayal. The actress playing her had none of Lauren's sparkle, but that's a trifling matter; more unsettling was the depiction of her phone call to me. In the movie, her voice is shaky and she's fighting back sobs. That's not my Lauren. The message she left was brave and resolute. But as I had told the families at our initial meeting with Greengrass, we had to let him make the movie his way. In the end, he did a superb job. I let go of my quibbles about how Lauren was depicted because, ultimately, *United 93* offered larger truths that needed to be told.

Five dozen family members turned out for the public premiere at the Tribeca Film Festival in New York City. The theater was walking distance from Ground Zero. It was surreal to stroll the red carpet, surrounded by movie stars and exploding flash bulbs. The families were given a special seating area in the balcony of the theater. When the movie ended, someone behind me began wailing. Maybe they hadn't made it to one of the preview showings, or maybe the movie hit them particularly hard this time, but this poor woman's crying was so loud and anguished it sent a chill through the whole theater. We were all frozen in our seats. Then this very sparkly crowd stood as one and turned to the balcony. The ovation was thunderous.

9

It took a while, but I finally started dating again. I was lonely. But my heart remained damaged, so I guess it's no surprise that none of the relationships were particularly healthy or happy. The most long-lasting of them was with a woman named Lisa. She felt haunted by Lauren's memory and was uncomfortable when I mentioned her, so I retreated into myself, still silently mourning Lauren while trying to find happiness with another woman I did not love.

Sleepy little Marin County isn't an easy place to be a bachelor because there is very little nightlife. Thankfully, Nick Graham created his own private club in a converted old office space. This speakeasy came to be known as the BBC. Local musicians would jam there and a bunch of us would regularly gather to hang out. One night in January 2006, I went to the BBC with some of the guys. At the little bar area, I fell into a quick conversation with Sarah Hopkins, a beautiful British lass whose elegant accent belied a bawdy sense of humor. We had a nice chat, and she certainly made an impression on me.

Over the next six months, Sarah and I crossed paths a few more times. I was separating from Lisa and Sarah had just ended a long relationship and was enjoying the freedom of being newly single, so nothing came of these chance encounters. We would regularly see each other at the BBC, and we had a great energy and always made each other laugh. One night that summer, Sarah was at the BBC with an old friend. He had been watching us interact and when she returned, he said, "Why aren't you and Jack together? You clearly have a special connection." Shortly thereafter, Sarah was at sushi with a dear girlfriend when my name came up in conversation. Her friend said she also noticed a great chemistry between us and encouraged Sarah to reach out. She texted me a sweet note and that led to our first date.

I was entranced from the very beginning. Sarah grew up in Norfolk, England, in a family of artists. She was the gentlest of souls, having dedicated much of her life to working on animal welfare causes. When we met, she was working for Guide Dogs for the Blind and had her own business doing pet illustrations in pencil and watercolor. Later, she landed her dream job at Marin Humane, our local animal shelter, working in animal services and veterinary medicine. Not for nothing, tattooed on the back of her left shoulder in fancy script is *There's no excuse for animal abuse*. Sarah turned out to be one of the most open and empathetic people I'd ever met. On our second date, she asked me many questions about Lauren and encouraged me to talk freely about her. It felt like a crushing weight suddenly lifted.

"I never felt threatened by Lauren's memory," Sarah says. "I understood that she would always be a big part of Jack, so I wanted to know more about this wonderful woman. I understood intuitively if I was going to be part of this journey he was on, then Lauren had to be a part of it, too. It was a package deal."

Sarah brought a lot of heart into my life and a lot of laughter. We had been dating for four months when New Year's

Eve rolled around. We agreed that we didn't have to be together, so I maintained the tradition of attending a gathering of friends that Sean Penn and Robin Wright hosted at their house, while Sarah told a group of her English friends that she would attend their "Vicars & Tarts" party. It's a British thing: the women dress like they're working in a bordello and the men come as louche priests. We thought it would be fine to not be together, but as the evening wore on, we both felt an urgent need to kiss at midnight, so around 11:30 Sarah came my way. She rings the buzzer at the front gate and Robin checks the security camera and here is this woman she had never seen before who is dressed like a hooker. I tell her that she's my date, in costume, and Robin says, "It better be, or you and Sean have some explaining to do." We still giggle about that one.

Sarah and I enjoyed the little things, like staying in and cooking a good meal, and I was delighted to have someone with whom to travel, so we went on memorable trips to Mexico, Puerto Rico, and the Cayman Islands. I love to scuba dive; being underwater, immersed in an entirely different world, soothes the soul. It says something about Sarah's generosity of spirit that she is afraid of the water but always insisted we go to tropical places so I could dive. In a lot of ways, we brought out the best in each other. "Jack is a classic gentleman who was taught wonderful manners by his parents," Sarah says. "If I get up at the restaurant to use the toilet, he stands up when I leave and again when I return. He always puts his jacket around me when I'm cold. I had never been treated with such respect in public. He raised the bar for me. In the past, whenever I would fight with a boyfriend, I would storm off, just run and hide. Jack taught me a lot about patience and communication. Because of his loss, he always had so much perspective. I remember one time we got kind of snippy with each other in the morning before I went to work. It wasn't about anything meaningful. By the time I arrived at work he had sent me an email that began, 'My darling Sarah, know that I always love you, we simply struck a wrong chord in our song of love this morning.' How can you still be mad when you read something like that?"

It felt wonderful to fall in love again, but it was also complicated. At times I felt tortured by guilt, like I wasn't supposed to be happy with someone else. Intellectually I knew this made no sense and that Lauren would want me to move on and find joy, but the feeling was very real. Sarah also had to wade through mixed emotions. One time we were on a double-date and when I was out of earshot, my friend's wife whispered to Sarah, "Don't expect Jack to ever marry you because Lauren was the one."

Says Sarah, "There were other comments like that along the way. There were many times I felt I wasn't good enough, or I was made to feel that way."

Yet we both always had this sense that Lauren was watching over us. "There was one evening when my best friend, Maryann, and I were drinking wine and talking," Sarah says. "Lauren came up in conversation, and I relayed Jack's comment that under different circumstances he thought Lauren and I would have been best friends. Just then the smoke detector started beeping. We weren't cooking or doing anything else that could have set it off. I had to fan the smoke detector to get it to stop. Maryann and I kept talking. Maybe ten minutes later I said that I felt that both Lauren and my late mother had helped bring Jack and I together. At that moment the fire alarm went off again. I got goosebumps. It felt like Mum and Lauren were talking to us."

On Lauren's birthday one year, I was feeling particularly nostalgic, so I decided to watch the video of her skydiving. I was excited to show it to Sarah for the first time. But the tape wouldn't play, even though I'd never before had trouble with my VCR. I kept trying and trying—it became very important to me to see the video and I was quite frustrated it wouldn't work. Suddenly the overhead lights flickered. It was as if Lauren was telling us, *Hey, don't worry, I'm just happy you're thinking about me.*

For Sarah, the connection to Lauren transcended these little moments. "I'm a very spiritual person," she said, "and I could feel Lauren's presence. Jack was still in the thick of things, he was still very much a troubled soul, and I could feel Lauren encouraging me to love him. Even more than that, I could feel her wanting to love him *through* me. I could feel Lauren's spirit directing me to caress him, to love him and comfort him."

Sarah writes poetry and felt inspired to put these feelings down on paper. One of her works brought me to tears. This is the final stanza:

She dwells on earth as light to buoy your spirit
Sharing your pain and laughing with you in your joy
You go on with your mortal life and celebrate hers
Because that would have been her wish
Do not mourn your flower and the bud within her belly
They are pollen on the breeze, rain on the new soil
Wind in the trees and the fire that drives you to go on

I was lucky to have found such a caring soul, but part of me was still trying to sabotage the relationship. Hanging out with Sean and Nick and others, I was partying pretty hard. I wanted to show people that even though I was the guy who lost his wife on United 93, I could still have a good time. I hated to feel pitied, so I tried to make every situation light and breezy. And the drinking allowed me to forget. It helped me drown out what I was feeling, or at least numb it. Back then I was having really sad dreams, many involving Lauren; often in these dreams we would be having a joyous time together and then she would abruptly disappear. I couldn't have articulated it at the time, but I was drinking myself to sleep at night hoping to keep the nightmares away.

Initially, Sarah accepted me for how I was, but over time the drinking got worse and as we became closer, she began to voice her concerns. I always made light of it, saying that I just liked the taste of good red wine. But it became such a source of conflict between us that Sarah told me a couple of times she was on the verge of walking away. I wooed her back with promises I never quite kept. I was hurting her and myself. One time a friend said to me, "Jack, you need to slow down or you're gonna kill yourself."

In the aftermath of that conversation and some tough talks with Sarah, I realized the depression had crept back in. One trigger was leaving my job at the Newspaper National Network, where I had been since 1995; I had a new boss I didn't love, the industry was changing, and I wasn't enjoying the work anymore. It was certainly a big lifestyle change to not go to an office every day for the first time as an adult. I also fundamentally misunderstood depression. I had beaten it once, so I thought I was cured forever, but that's not how it works; self-care and vigilance are necessary to keep it at bay. What I did know was that I needed to lean on the people around me. When you're in the depths of despair, it's very isolating but you're never alone. There are always people who love and care for you, it just takes strength and courage to ask for help. Sarah was my rock. I was (and still am) amazed at her ability to love unconditionally. "I always thought I was looking for a perfect man," Sarah says. "What I learned is that love is not about perfection, it's about being able to navigate imperfections together. We saw the potential in each other, but it was a lot of hard work to get through our stuff."

I started coaching the golf team at Marin Catholic High School, which was such a fun and rewarding experience; the positive energy of the kids did so much for me. As I took better care of myself, I emerged from the darkness, which allowed me to be a beacon of hope for Sarah when she went through her own crisis. In the span of a couple of weeks in 2009, she was laidoff from her job at Guide Dogs for The Blind and served an eviction notice at the beautiful little cottage where she had lived for eight years. We had been together for three years at that point, about the same duration at which four previous relationships of hers had ended. "Everything hit me at once," Sarah says. "I felt so unsteady and couldn't see the future at all. I was having panic attacks and crying every morning. I became really withdrawn. I suffered horrible social anxiety and Jack was always having to cover for me, saying I was sick. He was quite bewildered by my behavior."

Eventually Sarah saw a therapist and was diagnosed with major clinical depression. "That woke up Jack," she says. "Because of his own experiences, he dug in his heels and was really there for me, because he finally understood what I was going through." Continued therapy helped rebalance Sarah. She began doing more animal portraits, making a living out of her passion. I wasn't ready yet to have her move in, so I helped her find another nice place to live. Things seemed better until her psychiatrist prescribed an anti-depressant to which Sarah had a bad reaction. On one of the first nights after she began taking the new medication, she called me in a panic. She had pulled out some of her hair and had thoughts of harming herself. I was running to the car to speed over to her apartment, but she insisted I stay at home, saying she needed space to work through it on her own. With some misgivings, I did as she asked. What I didn't know was that Sarah then turned off her phone and went to bed.

"At six in the morning there was a pounding at my front door," she said. "Jack had been calling and calling, and when I didn't answer he lost it. I'll never forget his face when I answered the front door. It was such a mix of fear and relief. He said, 'Oh my God, I thought you'd killed yourself.' We held each other tightly for a long time, feeling how much we meant to each other." With the help of a new doctor, Sarah quickly found a medication that worked. She emerged from her depression stronger and healthier and has never looked back.

This was a real turning point for us and made me want to show a deeper commitment to her. I had told Sarah early on that I didn't think I'd ever get married again. She was accepting of that, but as time went on, she understandably wanted a tangible sign of my dedication to her. As it turned out, I had the perfect ring.

A couple of weeks after 9/11, I received a call from a local jeweler asking when I planned to come by. I had completely forgotten that for Lauren's birthday we took in her wedding ring to have a few new stones added. Retrieving the ring was bittersweet. I was glad to have something to hold on to that reflected our love, but it also became another symbol of loss. The ring had been sitting in a safe ever since the day I reclaimed it from the jeweler. Recognizing the potentially fraught emotions,

I asked Sarah how she would feel about wearing Lauren's ring. "I was honored," she says now. "I knew the significance of that ring. I thought it was incredibly meaningful that Jack wanted it on my finger." It was not an engagement ring, just my way of promising to love and care for Sarah.

Even that came with shadows. I had never been a worrier, but it was becoming a problem with Sarah. If she didn't return my call or text quickly, I would keep trying until I reached her and knew she was okay. One time at the gym I saw Sarah hug a guy and I got pretty upset. It made no sense—she has always been a hugger and I had no reason to doubt her love for me. But there were other incidents like that and I realized that what I was experiencing was a fear of abandonment. My therapist helped me to understand that I saw any male attention to Sarah in the same context as the hijackers on United 93: they were a threat to take away a woman I loved. I wasn't there to protect Lauren and now I was becoming consumed with watching over Sarah. It took some work, but I learned to let go of those fears. Still, they were yet another reminder that even as I was trying to start a new life more than a decade after 9/11, I was still haunted by my loss.

With this as the backdrop, my drinking continued. It took someone from outside my inner circle to give me the tough love I needed, and it came in the unlikely form of Frank Brickowski, the six foot nine former NBA player. He's a friend of a friend and we all wound up hanging out together at the 2013 Pebble Beach Pro-Am, during which I got bombed a couple of times. Frank has seen a few things and he recognized that this was not just a good time that went a little too far. He's a pretty intimidating guy and he got in my face and said, "You need to get your shit together." He insisted I reach out to a therapist and, ultimately,

I was referred to a specialist in EMDR psychotherapy. I had never heard of it.

Turns out EMDR is a therapy that is increasingly used to treat what has traditionally been called PTSD, but I prefer to use the emerging acronym PTSI; the *I* stands for *injury* rather than a *D* for *disorder*. It is a small but important distinction that will hopefully reduce the stigma attached to PTSI. In EMDR therapy, the patient discusses their trauma while the therapist constantly redirects their field of vision, engaging both hemispheres of the brain simultaneously and building new pathways for thought and emotion. I had been struggling for so long I was willing to try anything. "You're burying something and we're going to have to figure out what it is," my therapist told me in our first conversation. The EMDR unlocked things deep within me. I went twice a week, and on one of these days I would also receive counseling for my drinking. It was easy to bring that under control once I began to address the underlying causes. Through EMDR the revelation came: for all these years I had been mourning Lauren without fully grieving for the baby we lost.

Over the years that child grew up in my mind, growing older every year. Whenever I would meet a new boy or girl, or see a friend's kids, I would compare their ages to how old my child should have been. This would always leave me despondent, but I just buried the feelings, time after time. Now, thanks to EMDR, I knew I would not be able to move on until saying goodbye to the baby I never got to hold. I didn't know how to do that, but my therapist left me thunderstruck by pointing out that Lauren's ashes also contained DNA of the child.

Ever since the wooden urn arrived from Shanksville, I had left the ashes untouched. I couldn't say why but something always stopped me from spreading them. Now I knew the time had arrived, but I still didn't know where to do it. Shortly after that breakthrough EMDR session, I recalled a day many years earlier when I was flying from Los Angeles to San Francisco. I had decided to call my mother from the airplane. I was telling her that I didn't know where or when to spread Lauren's ashes. At that moment, the phone went dead and the plane banked right. I was sitting by the window and looked out to see the coast of Big Sur. It was as if Lauren was answering my question, pointing me to let her rest on the beautiful beaches below. It just took me a few years to figure that out.

A few days after my last EMDR therapy, I journeyed to one of Carmel's beaches to spread the ashes. I spent a long while taking in the incomparable beauty and then it was time to set free Lauren and our child. What I didn't know is that after so many years the ashes had compacted. Nothing was coming out of the upturned urn, no matter how hard I shook it. Finally, a few chunks of ash broke free but there was also a strange rattle. Four metal rivets. From the airplane. They had been cremated along with Lauren's remains and all this time remained embedded in the ashes. I was so shocked I fled the beach.

Those little rivets sent me to a dark place. It was a graphic reminder of the blunt force trauma that had ended Lauren's life. It took me a few months and more conversations with my therapist before I was ready to try again to spread the ashes. This time I took out the urn ahead of time and placed the ashes in a plastic container, taking great care to ensure no more shrapnel from the plane remained. I also brought with me the ashes of Nicholas the cat, so Lauren could be reunited with her beloved kitty. Before heading to the beach, I went to visit my dad in Carmel Valley. But his dementia had advanced, and it was an upsetting visit. I wasn't in the right frame of mind as I headed to the beach, and then I heard Lauren's voice in my head: *Go to Mission Ranch and have a Tanqueray and tonic and enjoy the view*. That was Dad's favorite drink. I followed that advice, and a peaceful feeling came over me. I made my way to the beach in time to catch a beautiful sunset. It's a very special place at the mouth of Carmel Valley, where the river runs to the sea. This time I spread the ashes without a hitch. I took some photos to send to Lauren's family and felt a profound sense of relief. The warm breeze was like an embrace, and I knew that Lauren was finally at peace. As I turned to leave the beach, I spotted a little sign in the sand bank on the edge of the dunes, two small pieces of wood in the shape of a cross emblazoned with SENSITIVE AREA. All I could think was, *Man, is it ever*. It had been a hell of a battle, but I'd finally said all of my goodbyes. At long last I was ready to start living again.

10

SOMETIMES THE BIGGEST SHIFTS in your life begin with the smallest observations. In May 2016, Sarah was flossing her teeth in front of a mirror when she noticed one of her tonsils was slightly enlarged. It's the kind of thing I would have blown off, but she went to see a doctor, who shared her concern and ordered a biopsy. The subsequent diagnosis hit us like a thunderbolt: cancer.

Instead of getting the comfort she needed, Sarah found herself taking care of me. I was so overwhelmed at the thought of losing her my PTSI kicked in and I spent the day after the diagnosis in bed, on Xanax. As always, Sarah was a trooper. "I didn't mind caring for Jack," she says. "Actually, it was quite helpful. It gave me something to focus on beside my own fears."

Luckily, we had caught the cancer in its early stages. Sarah went in for major surgery only a few weeks after first spotting the bump. Her devoted sister, Debbie, spent the first forty-eight hours after the surgery taking care of her, even sleeping on a couch in Sarah's hospital room. She never left her side. Three weeks after the surgery, we received clear pathology results, which was a huge relief. I rallied to help Sarah with the arduous recovery process. Her neck muscles had been damaged as part of the surgery, which involved removing all of the lymph nodes on the left side. She needed extensive physical therapy just to be able to lift her head off a pillow or raise her arm above her shoulder. She also required speech therapy and had to relearn how to swallow due to the wide-margin tonsillectomy performed to remove the cancer. Sarah was so brave, and it felt great to finally be there for her when she needed it.

On one of our first walks after Sarah's surgery, I blurted out that I wanted to marry her. It was a spontaneous comment, but the feeling had been bubbling up inside of me for a while. Sarah was taken aback and later confided that she thought I was just feeling sorry for her. But being confronted with the awful possibility of losing her made me want to hold on to Sarah even tighter. We had already been a couple for more than a decade and were living together so the only way to further show my devotion was to give her a proper wedding. Of course, I took my sweet time about it, but on May 24, 2018—two years after her cancer diagnosis—I got down on one knee and popped the question at Spanish Bay Beach. Sarah was so surprised she said, "You're kidding, right?"

I assured her that I wasn't. She broke down with joyful tears, said, "Yes!" and then she did the cutest happy dance atop the picnic table where we were sitting.

As part of our fresh start, we decided we needed a new nest. When Sarah moved into my house, she did her best to add a feminine touch, but I think it always felt more like mine than ours. We both loved the idea of moving to Pebble Beach and we found a bright, airy beach house near Spanish Bay. That fulfilled a dream of mine going back to when I was a boy watching the Crosby Clambake on television with my dad.

In his final years, Monterey Peninsula Country Club is where we spent a lot of our time. One of our last rounds of golf together was played there on December 20, 2011, on a beautiful, crystal clear day. Dad was eighty-seven and already suffering from dementia but there was still a lovely rhythm to his golf swing. On the ninth hole of the Shore Course, a tough par 3, I hit a good tee shot but lost the flight of the ball in the brilliant glare of the sun. Up near the green, on the other side of 17 Mile Drive, there is a scenic turnout and one of the drivers started honking his horn. What he knew, but I didn't, was that my ball had trickled into the cup for my first (and still only) hole in one.

Dad didn't quite comprehend the magnitude of the moment, so I had to call my good friend Mike Collins. I shouted out the news and he peppered me with questions.

"How long was it playing?"

"One hundred and eighty-six yards."

"What club did you hit?"

"Five iron."

"What kind of ball was it?"

"Titleist 5."

"Who were the witnesses?"

"Just my dad."

A pregnant pause.

"So, you make your first hole in one and your only witness is a senile eighty-seven-year-old man?"

"Screw you, I made an ace fair and square. And there was another witness, but I didn't get his license plate number."

Sadly, soon after we had to move my dad into an assisted living community. His cognition continued to deteriorate and taking care of him was too heavy of a burden for my mom. Dad stabilized in his new environment. I would visit him often, bringing him dark chocolate, which always seemed to perk him up. On one occasion he was clever enough to crack the door code and escape. I thought he'd only last four months there but this tough former marine lasted four years. Dad finally passed on December 7, 2016, at the age of ninety-three.

~

ON THE EVENING OF September 11, 2019, Sarah and I took flowers to Lauren Place, a lovely courtyard in San Rafael, California, that the city dedicated to her on the first anniversary of 9/11. It's situated on Fourth Street, between a fitness center and a nice restaurant, which always makes me smile because Lauren loved to both eat and exercise. There is a bronze plaque commemorating her life. Every 9/11 I take flowers and there are often dozens of other bouquets, placed by old friends and perfect strangers who have never forgotten one of the city's favorite daughters. This time around, as Sarah and I walked toward the courtyard to tidy up the flowers and light candles, we were holding hands and chatting about our upcoming wedding. I made the comment that I hoped Lauren would approve. Just then the streetlight above us started blinking off and on. We laughed knowingly. There was Lauren, watching over us yet again.

Seventeen days later we were married. The date was intentional. Ever since 9/11 a part of me dreaded the arrival of September and all the heavy emotions and remembrances that came with it. Now flipping the calendar to our anniversary month would be a joyful new tradition.

The wedding was a small gathering of four dozen of our closest friends and family. Sarah could not have looked more radiant. When I finally laid eyes on her, as she entered the courtyard in her elegant, sexy gown, my eyes welled with tears. I could tell she was overflowing with joy, too.

"I never expected to be a bride at the age of fifty-three," she says. "I couldn't believe how nervous I was. All the years we were together I told myself, and other people, that we were happy just as things were, but deep down I always hoped and dreamed of being Jack's wife and having a beautiful, romantic wedding. For me it was the missing piece of the puzzle. Having that dream come true was really powerful. It felt like I was a tree that had been growing in a big pot and suddenly I was being planted in the ground."

Nick Graham officiated the ceremony and offered a brilliant riff on the meaning of life and love, going all the way back to the creation of the universe. "The chances that matter would come together as it did to create life as we know it are one in a trillion," he said. "Sarah and Jack, this stardust has come together to create who you are at this moment. There is no one else like you and never will be again. The journey to get to this place has taken billions of years and a remarkable set of circumstances that will never be repeated.

"This marriage is the result of a star exploding and a galaxy forming long ago. The light we will see when we open our eyes will be the same as it was fourteen billion years ago. But this light will be slightly different now. This light will be brighter and warmer; it will be the light from the beginning of Sarah and Jack's journey, and from this day forward we will always be expanding and growing with them."

Sarah and I wrote our own vows, which were filled with humor and sentiment, just like our life together. The reception afterward was very romantic and also quite lively. My mom, still spry at ninety-one, gave a cheeky toast entitled "At Last," during which she drew lots of laughs making fun of how long it took me to ask for Sarah's hand. "Can you imagine if they waited thirteen more years?" Mom asked. "They would likely be late for their own wedding as Sarah is looking for her hearing aid and Jack can't find his teeth. As they start the ceremony, the big guy asks, 'Do you take this man to be your lawful wedded husband?' And Sarah asks, 'Awful what?' After the sweat of Jack's bald head gets blotted, they then kiss and exchange canes. Following a sumptuous dinner of soft food served in elegant large bowls, everyone toasts the bride and groom with mugs of warm milk." This went on for a while and finally Mom said, "Jack and Sarah thank you for not waiting any longer."

Our first dance as a married couple was the acoustic version of "Songbird" by Eva Cassidy. Sarah and I couldn't take our eyes off one another. The next dance was something else entirely, set to "She Sells Sanctuary," the classic rock anthem by The Cult. This tune has always made me think of Sarah because she really has been my sanctuary. One lyric really resonates: *And the fire in your eyes keeps me alive*. On the dance floor we cut loose, particularly me. I don't think I've ever danced like that in my life. "He went a little nuts," Sarah says. "I asked him afterward, 'Jack, what the heck got into you?' I could tell there was some big stuff going on. He told me he felt like a huge weight had finally been lifted after eighteen years. He had always been the 9/11 guy who had never gotten married again. Suddenly he felt free and light and just wanted to throw himself around. That's some of the most emotion I've ever felt from him, that lightness and happiness. I could see in his eyes he was really, really proud to be where he is now.

"What a journey it's been. But we made it. Together."

11

LAUREN'S PRESENCE REMAINS TANGIBLE. My mom still keeps a photo of her by the bed, which she consults for advice. Mom swears to this day that fifteen years ago, while making her hundredth scuba dive, she saw Lauren lounging on a coral reef, her beautiful hair flowing in the currents. She gave Mom a thumbs-up and swam off. In my youth I might have made fun of this. Now? I'm willing to admit there are things about life and death for which I'll never have all the answers. Mom's vision is real to her, and that's all that really matters.

Lauren lives on in other ways. I have a handful of friends who have brought new life into this world in the birthing room named for Lauren at Marin General Hospital. In downtown Houston, where Lauren went to high school, there is a memorial park dedicated to her in Old Market Square. James Baker, President George W. Bush's chief of staff, helped preside over the dedication on September 11, 2011. It's a peaceful place to visit and remember all who perished on 9/11.

Lauren is also memorialized on the warship USS *Somerset*. (That is the name of the county in Pennsylvania where Shanksville is located.) The area where amphibious landing craft exit the ship is ringed by the names of those who died on

United 93, and hers carries a special notation: *Lauren Catuzzi Grandcolas and Unborn Child.* The *Somerset* often comes to San Francisco for Fleet Week and I've visited it a couple of times to meet the brave men and women who are protecting our freedom. It's quite humbling to hear their stories and feel their reverence for those aboard United 93, who they rightfully consider the first heroes in the war on terror. In 2019, I took my friend Rick Kimball aboard the USS *Somerset.* He's been very successful in the business world and seen and done a lot of things, but Rick was overwhelmed at the sight of Lauren's place in that ring of honor. He broke down a couple of times and later told me it was one of the most moving experiences of his life.

Lauren's legacy can also be found on Amazon.com. In the months before 9/11 she had been working on the book she had long dreamed about, a self-empowerment guide for women in their thirties and forties. Her sister, Vaughn, and I decided we needed to bring the book to life, so we gathered all of Lauren's work and in 2005 it was published under the title *You Can Do It!: The Merit Badge Handbook for Grown-Up Girls.* The proceeds go toward the charitable foundation in Lauren's name. It's a really clever book: 512 pages full of encouragement for women to dust off old dreams, overcome their inhibitions, and finally achieve long-held desires. There is practical advice and step-by-step instructions (and some kick-up-the-backside pep talks) on everything from starting a business, going back to school, speaking in public, learning to play a musical instrument, and even changing a flat tire. The book brims with Lauren's optimism and love for life.

I'm still reminded of these qualities in little ways. I always held on to boxes full of Lauren's old letters, photo albums, diaries, and other mementos. Every now and then I'd have occasion to go through them and new treasures always revealed themselves. Lauren was a habitual list-maker. One day I came across a notebook of hers in which she jotted down a whimsical list of things entitled "Things that make me happy":

1. *Daylight saving time*
2. *Dancing wild*
3. *Fred Astaire in anything*
4. *Great sex*
5. *Music boxes*
6. *Bathing w/bubbles*
7. *Babies*
8. *Old pictures*
9. *Talking with friends—good talks*
10. *A good cry*
11. *Lions*
12. *Head rubs!*
13. *Snow from a window*
14. *Swimming alone*
15. *Fires*
16. *Nice wine*
17. *This list*

I always safeguarded these mementos because of their personal meaning but I also knew that Lauren is part of a much larger story and they were important documents of what is now a public life. In 2020, I finally donated all of these personal affects to the National Park Service, which oversees the 9/11 Memorial in Shanksville. In speaking with a very compassionate curator named Betsy Keene, I mentioned that I had held on to the airplane rivets that tumbled out of the urn with Lauren's ashes. It felt weird to throw them away, but I didn't know what to do with them. Betsy told me there is a rock at the crash site where unidentified remains were buried. I sent her the rivets so they could be returned to the earth alongside the other shards of United 93. More closure.

The voicemail Lauren left me from aboard United 93 can still be heard in the 9/11 museum in New York City and at the memorial in Shanksville. To this day I still receive regular correspondence about Lauren, often from students who are first studying 9/11. Something in her story seems to resonate with kids. One thoughtful young man wrote to tell me he had chosen to do a report on Lauren and United 93 because one of his classmates referred to it as "the plane that didn't do anything." I knew what he meant. It's part of what drove me to write this book—I want the world to remember Lauren and understand the void that was left behind. There are now multiple generations of Americans who weren't alive on 9/11 or were too young to fully absorb its impact. Plenty of other folks have chosen to forget. A few years ago at an airport, after having gone through security, I was on a bench tying my shoelace next to a middle-aged woman doing the same. We locked eyes and she said, "9/11 sure turned out to be an inconvenience." The shock took my breath away. I needed every ounce of my composure to quietly say, "For some more than others."

That kind of ignorance and apathy is not uncommon and through the years it has forced me to reflect on the larger meaning of 9/11. What kind of merciful God would allow such a tragedy? To that haunting question I now have a simple answer: it wasn't God—yours or mine—that manifested 9/11. It was human ideology.

A week or two after Lauren died, when I was at my lowest, hunger drove me to the kitchen, where I was confronted by an empty fridge. I was so discouraged I just wanted to crawl back into bed, but I heard Lauren's voice in my head: *Go to the store, it will be good for you. Get some fresh air and take better care of yourself.* I did as I was told, even though I felt jumpy the whole time, afraid I'd run into someone I knew and have to actually interact. Walking down one of the aisles, I passed a young African American mom and her child. Just then, this lovely young mother asked her son if he wanted a certain type of cereal, to which the boy said he "hated" it. The mom admonished him gently, saying, "Hate is not a word we use. It's not something we feel. Let's try that again." I was so moved I wanted to hug her, and I had the strongest feeling that little encounter was the reason Lauren had sent me to the store. It crystalized for me that hate is something that must be taught. We're all born to love. No child has hate in his or her heart, they just want affection and care. The hate is taught later, and if it metastasizes it can turn airplanes into missiles. Lauren's life ended because of hate but her final moments were defined by something much more powerful. Her phone call to me from aboard United 93 was the ultimate expression of love, and those words will live on forever. Losing Lauren pushed me to the breaking point. Love is what saved me.

Afterword

JUNE 8, 2020, STARTED off as a pretty normal day during otherwise strange times. I was all alone at our place in Pebble Beach while Sarah was in San Rafael, getting things in order as we prepared to sell our home there. Another chapter was closing. Lauren and I had never lived together in that house, but it was in the town where we shared so many nice times. Moving away would be another way of moving on, allowing Sarah and I to start fresh together in a new place where all the memories would be our own. I had an afternoon tee time to play golf with my pals; the game had been a saving grace during the coronavirus pandemic, allowing me to get fresh air and exercise while enjoying competition and camaraderie in a safe, socially distanced environment.

After golf, my buddies Eric, Joe, Dan, and I picked up some dinner to-go from the club and came back to the house. Mindful of coronavirus concerns, we avoided any indoor settings and ate in the backyard, huddled around the big, circular, wood-burning fire pit. The evening fog crept in, and I got the blaze roaring to keep us warm. My friends offered to carry the dishes into the kitchen when we finished eating but I waved them off. I walked the guys out and then returned to the backyard. It was around 9:30 p.m. The fire was still going strong. I had a fleeting thought that I should douse it with a hose but decided against it, not wanting to smoke out the neighbors. I would let it burn out on its own. I gathered up all the plates, silverware, and wine glasses in one big armful. As I turned toward the house, I banged my shin on the stone edge of the fire pit. It hurt like hell and knocked me off-balance. To steady myself, I attempted to sit down on the wide lip of the pit. I misjudged my landing and ended up precariously balanced on the very inner edge, with my arms still full of dishes. The momentum carried me backward and I tumbled toward the flames. As I fell into the abyss, I had enough time for only one thought: *Oh, shit.*

When I landed at the bottom of the red-hot fire pit, my arms were pinned at my sides and my legs were up in the air. My torso was wedged in between a couple of big logs. I felt like a turtle on its back. I was trapped. Helpless. As I tried to wriggle free, the flames rose all around me as my clothes were consumed. Soon, my skin was ablaze, too. But I didn't feel any pain, I guess because my body had been flooded with adrenaline. The seconds ticked by and I became almost relaxed. I thought, *Lauren, if this is the end, show me the white light.* It never came. Instead, I saw in my mind's eye an image of the devil in profile, holding a tablet of names in the flames around me. He glanced my way and said, "Give it another minute and your soul will be mine." That was the jolt I needed to fight for my life. I shouted, "Oh, no it won't!" Suddenly a much more angelic vision came to me: Sarah's face. With all the strength left in my body I pulled an arm free, slammed my hand into the fiery logs and thrusted myself upward. At that moment, it felt like someone or something grabbed me by the scruff of my neck. I don't know if it was angels or Lauren's enduring spirit or the power of Sarah's love, but some otherworldly force propelled me out of the ashes. My tattered clothes were still on fire, so I rolled in the grass to extinguish the embers.

I knew I was in big trouble and made a snap decision: there wasn't time to wait for an ambulance. I went to the bedroom and slipped on pajama pants and a t-shirt and then, with great difficulty, squeezed into my little two-seater. Thankfully, the Community Hospital of the Monterey Peninsula is only minutes from the house, so I carefully drove myself there, leaning forward to protect my back. I parked right in front of the emergency room. An attendant hustled over to shoo me away, so I lifted my shirt. He recoiled at the sight. "Oh, my God," he said softly. "How were you able to drive yourself in that condition?!" Then he began shouting into a walkie-talkie. Next thing I knew I was on a gurney being rushed into the ER.

Once stabilized, I had only one thought for the nurses: "I have to call Sarah." But she had already gone to bed with her phone's ringer turned off.

It was quickly determined that my burns required special-ized care, so I was loaded into an ambulance for the seventy-mile drive to the Santa Clara Valley Medical Center. Heavily sedated, I lapsed in and out of consciousness throughout the journey. I vividly recall one vision of walking through a beautiful field surrounded by waterfalls. I felt engulfed by tranquility…until a faint voice broke the reverie: "We're losing him." I was just self-aware enough to realize that they were talking about me. I opened my eyes with a startle. The EMT hovered above me, holding a long needle. "You just adrenalized yourself," he said. He had been about to plunge in the needle to bring me back from death's door.

A gaggle of doctors and nurses were awaiting my arrival in Santa Clara. As I was being wheeled in, one doc asked if I knew my name. When I gave him the correct answer, he said, "Mr. Grandcolas, are you allergic to anything?"

Realizing these might be the final words I ever spoke, I figured I should go for one last laugh: "Just beautiful nurses."

With a smile, the doctor said, "Take this character in and get him prepped."

After surviving that first surgery, I spent the next thirty-three days in the ICU burn unit, which was its own kind of hell. I had third- and fourth-degree burns across almost the entirety of my back. Equally scorched were parts of my arms, upper legs, buttocks, and my right hand, which I had jammed into the burning coals to finally give myself the leverage I needed to rise from the fire pit. In all, I had burns across 18 percent of my body.

The first surgery debrided the burned tissue from the lesions. During the second surgery, my back was covered with donated skin from a cadaver, attached with 184 metal staples that would later have to be removed in a slow, agonizing process. After my initial surgery, a nasty E. coli infection raged and plunged me back to critical status. For two days I was on life support, needing blood transfusions and bag after bag of intravenous fluids and medicine. Thanks to the great medical care, I pulled through, and then it was time for the final surgery. My talented plastic surgeon, Dr. Deepak Gupta, first removed the cadaver skin and then, using a surgical implement called a dermatome, thin layers of skin were peeled from each of my legs, from knee to hip. This was then meshed and stretched to cover all the wounds and attached with another round of staples. Dr. Gupta had said my legs were going to hurt more than my back and he wasn't kidding. It was pain on top of pain, the likes of which I never could have imagined. Twice a day the wounds had to be cleaned and the bandages changed. I came to dread this excruciating ritual.

What made each day even tougher was being apart from my darling Sarah because the hospital's COVID protocols prevented her from visiting. I put on a brave face when we FaceTimed, but deep down I ached for her. In reflecting on what we call "the accident," I know now that what propelled me out of the cauldron was my burning love for Sarah. Just before I plunged my hand into the fire to lift myself up, an awful thought had run through me: if I didn't make it out, she would suffer the same pain I did from losing a spouse without being given the chance to say goodbye. More than my own desire to live, what saved me was wanting—needing—to spare Sarah that anguish. Still, those weeks in the hospital were tough on both of us. "Jack was on really heavy painkillers and when we FaceTimed I barely recognized him," says Sarah. "His pupils were dilated, and he had painful expressions I'd never seen before. I tried to be upbeat when we talked but as soon as we'd hang up, I would start weeping. It was so hard to see him like that. And he was really struggling with the isolation of being all alone in a small, claustrophobic hospital room day after day. My heart just broke for him."

My doctor told me that based on the severity of the burns he can usually estimate pretty accurately how long a patient will be hospitalized. He figured I'd be in for eight to ten weeks. That would not stand; I simply couldn't go that long without seeing Sarah. (And, honestly, the hospital food was terrible.) After my final surgery, I pushed myself hard in the recovery process. It was important to get my body moving and blood pumping, so if the physical therapist instructed me to walk down the hallway once I did it three times. Over the preceding few years, I had gone to kickboxing classes two or three times a week, so alone in my hospital room I dusted off some of those moves. I was sustained by the compassionate nursing care and the love of close friends, who called and texted constantly and, after hearing my bellyaching, had many tasty meals from local restaurants delivered to my room. Less than five weeks after my accident I was ready to be released from the hospital. Sarah was required to visit so the nurses could show her how to care for my wounds. Our first embrace was cinematic in its sweetness.

Ahead of her visit, Sarah asked me to send photos of my back and legs, so she could prepare herself emotionally for what awaited. Still, I was afraid for her to see me in the flesh.

Alone in the hospital room, I asked Sarah, "Do you still love me like this?"

"Even more," she answered.

Hearing that, I shed tears of relief.

"Almost losing Jack made me realize how much he's part of my life now," says Sarah, "in the same way he was made to feel that when I had cancer. I gained a whole new appreciation for what a remarkable man he is. To know how hard he fought to live, and the struggles and bravery it took to get through his recovery, I'm just in awe of his courage, strength, and stoicism."

～

WHILE I HAD BEEN fighting my own personal battle, the coronavirus crisis further engulfed the nation. When the pandemic first hit, I thought my fellow Americans might come together as they had in the days after 9/11, when we shared a common purpose. But the coronavirus only deepened our divisions. I was particularly affected by the wrenching stories of COVID patients who died alone in the hospital, unable to receive from their loved ones a hug or final farewell. I felt these losses so deeply because I had just experienced the profound loneliness of a hospital room, and I will always feel the void of not getting to say goodbye to Lauren.

As the coronavirus death toll surpassed half a million and just kept climbing, I couldn't help but think of the millions of family members left behind—half the bed cold and empty, or a seat at the dinner table that would remain forever unfilled. All of these deaths come with a massive wave of collateral damage, as the sudden loss creates deep emotional trauma in the survivors (which I consider a kind of mental injury). I know from experience that for those left behind the first year is the hardest. There are so many firsts that must be experienced: first Thanksgiving without your loved one, first Valentine's Day, first birthday, first wedding anniversary. It's like poison in your gut, and the pain pushes you toward isolation, loneliness, and despair. You have to battle hard to not be consumed by the darkness.

A couple of months after my accident, I ran into my friend Scotty from the golf club. A year earlier his son had died in a tragic accident. Knowing my own story of loss, he confided in me that he, his wife, and their other son were all struggling. I told him about the EMDR therapy that freed me from the sadness and survivor's guilt that had been my shadow for more than a decade after Lauren's passing. I hadn't spoken to this man since our initial conversation, and when I saw him again all those months later, he thanked me with great feeling for steering his family toward EMDR. They had all done the therapy and it helped bring them peace and acceptance amidst the grief. Through the years I have shared hard-earned advice with a few other folks in crisis and it gives meaning to losing Lauren.

But what to make of my own near-death experience in the fire pit? I'm sure plenty of people think I'm the unluckiest guy in the world. For a long time I bought into that, too, which was one of the reasons I waited so many years to propose to Sarah; I didn't want to jinx it. After she beat cancer, I thought my luck had finally changed. But as I continue to reflect on the highs and lows of the last two decades, I've come to realize that I am very lucky indeed. I found true love, twice. I've endured a pair of horrific tragedies but still have a resilient spirit and zest for life. I'll always carry the emotional scars of losing Lauren and our child, just as I'll always have the physical scars from my burns, but all of my wounds continue to heal.

We all suffer loss. We all endure heartbreak. It's how you respond to these cataclysms that define you. Sometimes the most beautiful things grow out of our hardest moments. I'm reminded of this every time I glance into the backyard. The fire pit is no more, having been turned into a planter box where the flowers bloom again and again.

End